Praise for *What Every Christian Needs to Know About Judaism*

"Rabbi Moffic creates a feast for the mind and heart, as he sets the table for a rich Passover experience. Historical events, biblical texts, and stories from Jewish communities through the centuries make for an engaging read, inspiring readers to explore the richness of the Passover in their own homes."
—**Lynn H. Cohick**, Professor of New Testament, Wheaton College

"People everywhere are seeking a better way to live. Many have a faith tradition we call home—but sometimes moving outside that tradition helps us see resources we never knew were there. Through his stories and insight, Rabbi Evan Moffic shines the light of Jewish wisdom in a way that helps all of us find our way."
—**Christine Chakoian**, Senior Pastor, First Presbyterian Church of Lake Forest

"Rabbi Moffic is an engaging teacher who excels at communicating ancient truths for modern audiences. His insights into Hebrew scriptures and the Jewish heritage of the Christian faith will be a blessing to all who want to learn."
—**Steve Gillen**, Pastor, Willow Creek Community Church

"Evan Moffic is a rabbi, but he's also an extraordinary scholar and a teacher of the highest order. He can speak to us all, whatever our faith or culture. And he does it with grace, humor, and erudition. Such a guy."
—**Jim Kenney**, International Interreligious Peace Council, Interreligious Engagement Project, Common Ground

"Rabbi Moffic is one of the best young rabbis and scholars I have ever heard speak and teach about both Judaism and Christianity. His wit, his humor, and his deep knowledge about the Old Testament and early Christianity will give insight into Jesus' Jewish context, history, and character."
—**Newton Minow**, former chairman of the Federal Communications Commission (FCC), Vice-Chair Coi
Debates

Praise from *What Every Christian Needs to Know About the Jewishness of Jesus*

"Jews and Christians need to talk with one another, but to do this each must listen to the other side. Many Christian scholars today have made colossal progress in grappling with Jewish sources and in listening to the variety of Jewish communities. Evan Moffic has stepped up the listening skills needed by the Jewish community to the voice of the Christian community. How has he done this? By going to the very source of the Christian faith—to Jesus himself, the Jewish teacher of Galilee in the first century. Moffic has accepted the challenge of seeking to explain Jesus as one who is best understood by understanding him as a Jewish teacher rooted in the Tanakh and the Jewish traditions. Christians will not all agree with everything Moffic says, but they will say he has listened well. For that alone I am immensely grateful for this book."

—**Scot McKnight**, theologian, speaker, and best-selling author of *The Jesus Creed*

"Thank you, Rabbi Moffic! As a Christian and a Catholic priest, I am grateful for the intriguing look into the Jewish life of Jesus. As such, this book is a wonderful gift to Christians who seek to further the rich faith and culture out of which Jesus emerged."

—**Father Tom Hurley**, pastor, Old St. Patrick's Church, Chicago

WHAT EVERY CHRISTIAN NEEDS TO KNOW ABOUT JUDAISM

EXPLORING THE
EVER-CONNECTED
WORLD OF
CHRISTIANS
and JEWS

RABBI EVAN MOFFIC

Abingdon Press
Nashville

WHAT EVERY CHRISTIAN NEEDS TO KNOW ABOUT JUDAISM

EXPLORING THE EVER-CONNECTED WORLD OF CHRISTIANS AND JEWS

Library of Congress Cataloging-in-Publication Data

Names: Moffic, Evan, 1978- author.
Title: What every Christian needs to know about Judaism : wisdom and tradition of the Jewish faith / Rabbi Evan Moffic.
Description: Nashville : Abingdon Press, 2020. | Includes bibliographical references.
Identifiers: LCCN 2019027438 (print) | LCCN 2019027439 (ebook) | ISBN 9781501871498 (trade paperback) | ISBN 9781501871504 (ebook)
Subjects: LCSH: Judaism—Relations—Christianity. | Christianity and other religions—Judaism.
Classification: LCC BM535 .M564 2020 (print) | LCC BM535 (ebook) | DDC 296.02/423—dc23
LC record available at https://lccn.loc.gov/2019027438
LC ebook record available at https://lccn.loc.gov/2019027439

Ancient language fonts were developed in the public domain for scholars who comprise the Society of Biblical Literature, including SPTiberian for Hebrew, SPIonic for Greek, and SPAtlantis for transliteration

20 21 22 23 24 25 26 27 28 29—10 9 8 7 6 5 4 3 2 1

MANUFACTURED IN THE UNITED STATES OF AMERICA

To all of the rabbis and teachers—Samuel Karff,
Ronald Shapiro, Michael Sternfield, Greg Wolfe,
Isaac Serotta, Stephen Pearce, David Gelfand,
Michael Zedek, David Saperstein, and many
more—who taught, inspired, and led me into
this extraordinary calling

CONTENTS

INTRODUCTION

Imagine you step into a time machine and arrive in ancient Egypt. The year is 1500 BCE. You see the Nile River rolling through fertile fields. You see a city teeming with people. A few are men dressed in elaborate colorful tunics, sitting atop shining chariots. Others stand in booths in a market, hawking various foods and goods. In the distance you see a gleaming palace. There lives the pharaoh, the supreme ruler, revered by many as a god. The pharaoh's ancestors are entombed in magnificent rising pyramids you glimpse farther in the distance.

You decide to go and explore those pyramids. As you near them, you see hundreds of men at work. They are making bricks, transporting and stacking them. They are small and slender, marching in lines surrounding by stronger men with whips and horses. Their sad and haggard faces make you wince. When they finish working, you follow them. They walk a mile or so to their ramshackle homes. There they greet their wives and children. They have a small meal, perhaps tell their children a story, and sleep when the night falls.

The next day they get up as the sun rises. Some walk back to the pyramids and begin making bricks and mortar again. Others walk toward the Nile and work in nearby fields. They continue working in the hot sun, pushed and heckled by the larger men with whips and horses. The men you're watching seem resigned to their fate. They are slaves in the most powerful nation in the world.

If you saw this scene and had no idea how history would unfold, what would you think? Which group do you think would survive over the 3,500 years? Would it be this small group of slaves, malnourished and powerless to challenge their captors? Or would it be the glorious Egyptian nation, with its wealth, fertile land, pyramids, and global empire?

If you had no knowledge of the future, you would choose the Egyptians. Of course they would survive. They have everything going for them. They are the superpower of the ancient Near East. You would think little of that small group of slaves. Their lot in life is one of death and decline. They will remain enslaved until they die, powerless to fight their overlords.

But history turned out much differently. The empire of ancient Egypt is no more. The last pharaoh died thousands of years ago. The pyramids remain, of course. The Nile River rolls on. And the descendants of that small group of slaves survive—not just as individuals, but as a people. The children of those slaves become the Jewish people. The text they claim as sacred has destroyed empires, built wealth, and transformed the world. Their message that every human being is created in the image of God gave us the idea of human dignity and helped end slavery in the West and establish today's norms of human rights. Their religious beliefs gave rise, in turn, to two other major world religions.

This book unpacks Jewish teachings and beliefs. It does so with an eye toward guiding Christians interested in deepening their understanding and appreciation of Judaism. Knowing more about Judaism brings Christians closer to Jesus because Jesus lived and died as a Jew and consistently quoted Jewish Scripture and stories. When Christians learn about Jewish tradition and history, they see the Bible and the life of Jesus from a new and enriching perspective. As scholar Paula Frederickson puts it, "Despite a long and often unhappy history, the story of Jews and of Christians remains intertwined. The bridge between the two is the historical figure of Jesus."[1] And that historical figure of Jesus becomes more accessible and instructive when we explore Jewish traditions and wisdom.

I write as a rabbi who leads a synagogue, devoting most of my time to leading Jewish worship, teaching classes on Jewish topics, and officiating at weddings, funerals, and other sacred rituals. But since I began my rabbinical studies, I have had another mission: building bridges and engaging with people of all faiths. Some of my passion for this work comes from my own history growing up in a community in Texas filled with devout Christians. I felt inspired by the devotion and sense of service I witnessed among my Christian friends and neighbors. I felt pushed to commit more deeply to my own faith and relationship with God. And, I was constantly explaining Judaism to my Christian friends.

As an adult, I have officiated at weddings of hundreds of interfaith couples. The conversations I had with them (and often their extended families) explored the role of faith in their lives. The women and men I've performed marriages for had questions about God, holidays, raising children, the best ways to talk about God in their home, and so much more. In talking with interfaith families about such topics, my aim has not been to convert the Christian partner to Judaism. Rather, my aim is that everyone in the conversation—including myself—might find a closer relationship with God and a deeper understanding of the roots shared by Christians and Jews. And I hope that exploring the riches of the Jewish faith tradition can foster bonds focused not on the troubled history between Jews and Christians but rather on a future in which we share wisdom with one another.

JUDAISM AND YOU

Our investigation of Judaism begins with the Jewish approach to God. What do Jews believe about God? Why does God allow bad things to happen to good people? What do Jews say in prayer? We continue by looking at the sacred Jewish texts, holy days, and daily practices. We also explore what happens in a Jewish synagogue and home, and what Israel means today for Jews. We conclude by answering some of the pressing and timely questions people ask me about Jews and Judaism.

But this book is not just about Judaism and the Jewish people. It is about you. It highlights the morsels and insights of the great Jewish sages that can help you live a richer and more meaningful life. This book is not a description of Jewish life so much as it is an invitation to soak up the wisdom and traditions of Judaism, whether you are Jewish or not. Indeed, throughout this book's explorations, we'll focus on what people of all faiths can learn from Jewish wisdom and practices. In this way, our explorations riff on and respond to God's words to Abraham in the Bible: "All the nations of the world shall be blessed through you" (Genesis 12:3, author's translation). Some rabbis, over the ages, have interpreted that to mean Israel will bring blessings to the world or that nations that accept Jews will prosper. I think it might mean something simpler: that one needn't be Jewish to have one's life enriched by Jewish teaching, Jewish spiritual practice, and Jewish approaches to God and neighbor.

~~~~~~~~~~

1

GOD

~~~~~~~~~~

What is the sound of God's voice? Does it have a certain timber and vibration? Is it deep and powerful, perhaps like the voice of James Earl Jones? Is it light and lilting, like the voice of Reese Witherspoon, or throaty like Kathleen Turner? Well, to me the voice of God sounds like the voice of Rabbi Samuel Karff. He is the rabbi who led the congregation where I grew up and worshipped with my parents every week. As a child, I remember his sermons brimming with knowledge and wisdom. I both loved him and was in awe of him. His presence filled the sanctuary with dignity. And his voice made us dream, cry, and act.

Rabbi Karff came from a long line of distinguished rabbis. He also wrote scholarly books. He was universally respected in Houston by people of all faiths. He was the kind of person I still aspire to be.

One of Rabbi Karff's most compelling and memorable sermons came after a massive hurricane struck Houston in 1995—during which a bolt of lightning struck and set fire to the Karffs' home. Rabbi Karff and his wife, Joan, escaped, but his library and almost all of his other possessions were destroyed. Soon the newspaper featured the story of the Karffs' home's destruction. It raised the question of why—of all the homes in Houston—the hurricane would destroy that of one of the city's most beloved clergypeople.

In response this question, Rabbi Karff reminded us that he could not explain God's actions. He was as puzzled and troubled as others were. But as a rabbi, he also served as a "defender of the faith." He wrote:

> Our response when people asked "Why us?" was "Why not us?" In the days following the fire, I alternated between the belief that God had some purpose beyond my power to fathom and the conclusion that this fire was not God's will but the price of living in a world in which nature follows its natural course. I did feel God's presence that night and during the days to come in our survival, in the strength we received to carry on, in the love of those who embraced and nurtured us, and in my faith that God would empower us to derive a blessing even from this ordeal.[1]

He did not know all of God's ways. But he knew God's presence.

The different feelings Rabbi Karff articulated capture different Jewish approaches to God. Some Jewish texts, interested in illustrating God's power, suggest that everything happens for a reason; other Jewish writers focus on God as a mystery we can never fully comprehend; still other Jewish sources offer a more deist interpretation that God set the world in motion and then stepped back to let human beings shape its fate. Jewish theologies differ on many points, but fundamental to them all is the idea that that no human being can understand everything about God. We are human beings, and God is God, and our knowledge is ultimately limited by this difference.

As Rabbi Karff once said, "Life is not a puzzle to solve, but a mystery to embrace."[2] Accordingly, this chapter does not give definitive answers about what Jews believe about God. Rather, it offers an overview of the different ways Jews have approached God and tried to make sense of a world in which God is sometimes keenly felt but often ignored or rejected.

Some might wonder why we need to ask questions about God in the first place. God, we might say, is simply the Ruler of the Universe. God is all-powerful, and that's that. Others might think that what's important about Judaism are our ethical teachings, and that "God" is a figment of the imagination. Indeed, many modern Jews draw just that conclusion. But for most Jews, for most of our history, God is like the air we breathe. Our ancestors didn't debate God's existence. They lived by it. They lived *toward* God—and they also struggled with God and wondered about God and loved God.

WHAT IS GOD'S NAME?

The Hebrew Bible begins by giving us two names for God: Elohim and YHVH (יהוה). We include the Hebrew letters for the second name because the pronunciation is unknown. Some people have transliterated the Hebrew as Yahweh. But the Hebrew letters are all consonants. According to Jewish legend, the proper pronunciation was once known by the High Priest of Israel, but it was lost over the generations. When we encounter it in the Torah, we say Adonai, which means "My Lord." Some Jews also say HaShem, which means "The Name." We abbreviate it with the set of letters

YHVH, symbolizing the four Hebrew letters—*Yud, Hay, Vav, Hay.*

Elohim is used in chapter 1 of the first book of the Bible, known in Hebrew as Bereshit (which means "in the beginning") and in English as Genesis. YHVH is used in chapter 2. In subsequent chapters of the Torah the two names are used interchangeably. Other names also appear throughout the book. They include El Shaddai, Yah, and HaMakom. Each of these names has spiritual significance. But the two most important and frequent are YHVH and Elohim.

YHVH is God's proper name. It is like Evan or Rachel. It is used in the context of the particular relationship between God and the Jewish people. Elohim is the more universal name. It reflects our understanding of God as the creator of the universe and source of nature. We will look at each in turn.

YHVH (יהוה)

A proper name is a unique identifier. We are not always identified by our proper name. If your proper name is Lauren, for example, you might also be called "my cousin" or "my sister." But your proper name remains unique to you. יהוה is God's proper name. But as we have learned, the correct way to say it is unknown. No one knows the right way to pronounce יהוה because יהוה is simply a series of letters with no vowels. It's like the English letters CBRH. Without vowels, we do not know the right way to pronounce that series of letters. It could be cobra, cubrah, cah-bar-uh. Since no one knows the proper pronunciation, we may be pronouncing it incorrectly. We all know it feels like an act of disrespect if someone mispronounces our name, even if it is an honest mistake. We do not want to disrespect God in that way, so Jews today do not try to pronounce this name. What do we do, then, when reading aloud a biblical passage with יהוה? Sometimes we say HaShem and sometimes we say Adonai.

ELOHIM

God's proper name—יהוה—is not the only name by which we know God. In fact, it's not the first name the Bible gives us. The first is Elohim. It is the third word of the Torah— *Beresheet Barah Elohim*, which means "In the beginning God created." Elohim is a troubling name for God because it seems like a plural noun. Most Hebrew words that end with *-im* are plural. It is like the *s* at the end of English words. But the Torah comes from one God. We don't say, "In the beginning, *gods* created the heaven and the earth." Jews recognize and worship one God, not many. So why does this name for God take on the Hebrew plural form?

In fact, while this name of God *appears* to be plural, it isn't. We know Elohim is a singular noun because the verb connected to it (create) appears in the singular form. The same is true throughout the story. The noun Elohim functions grammatically in the singular. But the use of a seemingly plural name still has a purpose. The God of the Bible— Elohim—contains all the earlier *ideas* of God people once espoused. For example, the ancient Greeks believed in a sea god, a love god, a fertility god, and so on. But the Israelites believed the one God of the universe created all of the waters of the sea *and* the loving bond between human beings *and* the process by which we bring new life into the world and much more. In other words, the God whom readers of the Bible are about to meet is a God who encompasses all the attributes and actions previously associated with many gods. By seeming to use a plural noun, the Torah conveys this truth.

This clarification may seem unimportant. Who cares if a noun appears in the singular or plural form? It matters because the name symbolizes the creation of order in the universe out of chaos and competition. One of the first acts of Elohim is to bring order out of the *tohu v'vohu*, which is often translated as unformed and void. It is the Bible's way of describing the random forces of energy permeating the universe. God creates order out of that chaos. Similarly, the first name of God unites all the previous ideas of gods people once had. Order emerges out of disorder. An earth unformed and void became one with day and night, oceans and lands, fruits, vegetables, and human beings. God creates an ordered world.

GOD AND SCIENCE

By creating an ordered world out of chaotic darkness, God models one of our core human tasks: to create life and to sustain it. In other words, empowered by God—made in the image of God—we are to also create order from chaos. We create relationships out of individuals. We create families out of relationships. We create societies out of families. We create nations and civilizations out of societies.

Our primary way of doing this is language. We form relationships and create meaning through the words we use. God teaches us how to do so. How does God create light? According to the Torah, God *said*, "Let there be light," and there was light (Genesis 1:3). God speaks the world into being. God's words created the light. How does God form relationships with Abraham and Moses and the other prophets? God speaks to and through them.

The tradition of Jewish mysticism known as the Kabbalah elaborates on this idea. Jewish mystics believed everybody and everything in the world is part of God. God was, is, and will be everything. That's because every creation in the world is simply a variation of the letters of God's name. It is mathematically possible because a set of letters has many potential permutations. Those letters can be repeated and put in different orders. According the Jewish mystics, every human being—every grain of sand—is a different permutation of the letters of God's name.

This idea may seem far-fetched. And the teaching, to be clear, does emerge from mysticism—metaphorical, poetic, spooled out on a register different from the register of reason and argument. But recently, I've been thinking about the ways that this mystical teaching about creation is, in fact, not just "mystical"—it's also surprisingly compatible with science. In the 1950s, scientists James Watson and Francis Crick discovered DNA as the backbone of creation. The cells of every living being are made up of strands of DNA. And what is DNA? It is a series of letters: ATCG. These letters form strands that replicate themselves to create the blueprints of life. In other words, every creation is a series of letters. The world is created through words. Does that sound familiar? One of the twentieth century's great scientists—Francis Collins—was so intrigued by this connection between DNA and the creation of the world that he called DNA the "language of God."[3]

With this understanding, we might say creation—as described in the opening chapters of the Book of Genesis— is the language of God assembled into sentences and paragraphs. The Bible itself is the book containing those paragraphs. It all begins with Elohim creating order out of chaos through the use of language.

THE BURNING BUSH

Another name of God is revealed to Moses at the burning bush, a story recounted in Exodus 3. Moses, walking through the desert, hears a voice. (According to Jewish legend, the voice sounded like Moses's father.) That voice tells Moses he has to return to the Israelites in Egypt and secure their freedom from Pharaoh. Moses hesitates. And then he asks God, "What is your name?" God answers Moses, "*Ehyeh-Asher-Ehyeh*" (Exodus 3:14).

This extraordinary phrase still mystifies many readers; knowing its meaning is essential to appreciating a core Jewish belief. The meaning of the phrase *Ehyeh Asher Ehyeh* is "I will be what I will be." Many translations use the phrase "I am what I am." This translation, however, is not accurate—the Hebrew does not have a word corresponding to the English word *am*. No Hebrew word exists for the present tense of "to be." For example, if you were to translate the English sentence "The girl is here" you would use only two Hebrew words—*girl* and *here*. If you were to say "The girl was here," or "The girl will be here," you would need three Hebrew words, the additional word corresponding to "was" or "will be." The same logic applies to the sentence "I am." You would only need one word for that sentence—the word *I*.

But when speaking from the burning bush in Exodus 3:14, God uses the future tense! The word *ehyeh* is the future tense of "to be." God's name is "I will be what I will be." God is dynamic. God works through history. What God will do cannot be known—God **will be** what God **will be**—because God does not stop speaking to and through us. God's commitments do not change. God's covenant with Israel remains forever, as does God's love of mercy, love, lament, and much more. But God's actions are ever new. God calls out to each of us in every generation. God is always present to each of us, regardless of when we are alive and how old we are. God guides us into the future.

I once struggled to explain this idea to a Bat Mitzvah student. She confronted me with a challenge that would, over the years, become familiar. "Rabbi," she said, "I really don't believe in God. I can't imagine there's an old man with a long beard in the sky deciding everything in the world. This temple is fine, and I like the songs. But I really honestly don't believe in some all-powerful God." I knew Brina loved summer camp, so I asked her how she feels when she is outside camping. Do you look around and feel the presence of something bigger than you? I asked. "Yes," she replied. "I feel different. I feel calm. I love it. But I still don't believe in God."

I have to admit, when twelve-year-old Brina said all this to me, I felt like a failure as a rabbi. Was I not compelling and inspiring enough as a teacher? Why could I not convey the deep sense of faith I had and that I believe will shape Brina's life for the better? Had I failed the parents who entrusted me to deepen the faith of their children? But I've learned to embrace my congregants' questions and even their resistances—because they illustrate an openness to God's presence. The opposite of faith is not doubt. It is indifference. It is disinterest. And I've found that the most effective way to respond to questions is not dismissal, but engagement.

So I turned to a prayer called the Amidah, also known as the standing prayer because we traditionally stand up when saying it. The Amidah begins by acknowledging the "God of Abraham, God of Isaac, God of Jacob, God of Sarah, God of Rebecca, God of Leah, and God of Rachel." These are the biblical patriarchs and matriarchs. I pointed out to Brina that the prayer could have just said "God of Abraham, Isaac, Jacob," rather than "God of Abraham," "God of Isaac," and so forth. After all, the same God spoke to each of these figures. But each man and woman experienced God differently. Abraham had a personal relationship with God different from Sarah's. Rachel experienced God differently than Jacob. So the prayer says "God of Abraham," "God of Sarah," "God of Leah," because each of them experienced the same God in different ways.

"Brina," I said, "you have an experience of God. It may not be the same experience Abraham or Moses had. It may not be the same experience your parents have. It may feel confusing sometimes. But relationships grow over time. And the fact that you are thinking and struggling with God means you have a relationship with God."

Is how you see God today the same way you saw God at age four? Perhaps some elements persist. I know they do for me. Often I feel the same sense of trust and reassurance of a guiding presence in the universe that I felt when I was a kid. But my experience of God has also changed as I have seen God's distance, God's whimsy, God's delight, God's justice, God's mercy. There is, in God, unchanging timelessness, and in my experience of God, there is change and growth. So, God is, and from the perspective of human beings, God will be what God will be.

GOD'S ESSENCE

For the ancient Israelites, God's essence was too vast to capture in words. No human description can encompass God. Every description of God is only an approximation. It is only a glimpse of God. That idea is conveyed by the Torah in Exodus when Moses asks to see God. God replies, "Here is a place near me where you may stand on a rock. When I pass by, I will put you in a cleft in the rock and cover you with my hand until I have passed by. Then I will remove my hand and you will see my back; but my face must not be seen" (Exodus 33:21-23, author's translation). In other words, no living human beings—even Moses—can ever see God fully. As a physical being we can never know God's essence.

But even as we cannot describe God's essence, we do know that there is only one God. Deuteronomy 6 contains a verse known by almost every Jewish person. It is also a verse Jesus quoted in the Gospels. Many rabbis call it "the watchword of our faith." It reads, "Hear, Oh Israel, the Lord (YHVH) is our God, the Lord (YHVH) is one" (Deuteronomy 6:4, author's translation). Dozens of books have been written unpacking this one verse. It is one of the simplest and clearest statements we have about God. God is one. There is not a sea god and a distinct and different fertility god and a distinct and different love god, as there were in ancient Greece. One God encompasses all those parts of nature and existence.

That assertion of monotheism shaped the future of Judaism and the birth of other religions. Yet, other parts of the Torah suggest multiple gods existed. Consider the Song of the Sea found in Exodus, where the Israelites ask, "Who is like you, Oh God (YHVH) among the gods who are worshipped?" (Exodus 15:11, author's translation). In other words, the Israelites seem to acknowledge the worship of other gods. Shouldn't they have said, "Who is like You among the *false* gods that are worshipped?" Biblical scholars describe the ancient Israelite views as "monolatry." That is, ancient Israelites acknowledged that other people worship other gods, but the Israelite God is the greatest and most all-encompassing God. The difference between monotheism and monolatry is that monotheism says there is only one God in the world. Monolatry acknowledges that other gods may exist, but one God encompasses and is more powerful than them all. Over time—perhaps by the beginning of the Common Era—monotheism fully replaced monolatry among Jews.

As we can see in this discussion of monotheism and monolatry, the Hebrew Bible contains varied understandings of God. But one consistent theme is that God has emotions. Abraham Joshua Heschel, a leading twentieth-century philosopher, said the biblical God is a God of pathos. God gets angry. God gets jealous. God loves. Heschel distinguished the God of the Bible from what he called the Aristotelian God, the unmoved Mover, an impersonal force in the universe. The Israelite God is personal. We form a relationship with God. This relationship is captured by the word *brit*, which means "covenant." God invites us into that covenant, as we see the stories of the Bible.

Now, it is not a relationship of equals, as we saw with Moses only glimpsing God's back. As Rabbi Karff once told me, God is the senior partner. But our relationship with God is a real relationship, as we relate to God through language (prayer), deeds, and faithfulness. The Hebrew word often translated as "faith"—*emunah*—really means "faithfulness." A committed relationship is built by faithfulness to one another. We have faith that God's commandments and teachings are righteous and just. And God has faith that we will live by them. That faithfulness is often tested. But it persists through forgiveness and compassion. It is eternal. That is the idea conveyed in a verse from the biblical book Hosea. It is a verse recited at Jewish weddings and traditionally said during daily morning prayers: "I will betroth you to me forever. I will betroth you to me in righteousness and in justice, in steadfast love and in mercy. I will betroth you to me in faithfulness. And you shall know the LORD (YHVH)" (Hosea 2:19-20 ESV). Our relationship with God is personal and eternal.

If we have a personal relationship with God, do we therefore believe God is a person? Does God have a body? Again, Jewish tradition contains different views. The Bible speaks of God's outstretched arm, God's face, and God's back. In the Book of Exodus, the Israelite elders sit at God's feet. Yet, one of Judaism's most revered rabbis, Moses Maimonides, said that to imagine God in bodily form is idolatrous because it limits God and seeks to make God fit our human perceptions. The Bible speaks of God in human form in order to help us, with our limited language and knowledge, to imagine and move toward God. God is beyond all description and understanding. All we can truly say is that God is perfect unity. God has no beginning or end, in time or in space. Maimonides argued that the biblical passages describing God's feet and arms are allegorical.

If the Hebrew Scriptures help us know God through metaphor, they also help us know about God through the choices and decisions God made. For example, God chose to give all people free will. Near the beginning of the Torah God says to Adam and Eve's son Cain, "If you do what is right, will you not be accepted? But if you do not do what is right, sin is crouching at your door; it desires to have you, but you must rule over it" (Genesis 4:7). Cain can choose whether to do good or evil. Like all human beings, Cain has free will.

Does this human free will limit God's power? Not according to the Jewish sages. Various explanations seek to reconcile human free will with God's omnipotence. Some suggest free will is a useful illusion, and from our limited human perspective, we have free will, but truly everything happens at the behest of God.

Another prominent explanation is that God intentionally limits God's own power in order to allow human beings to choose good or evil. A Jewish mystical text called the Zohar calls this process *tzimtzum*. It means "contraction." God voluntarily contracts from overt involvement human affairs in order to allow human beings to exert their freedom. This was not always the case. During the period of the Bible, God was active in history. God inflicted the plagues on Egypt. God split the Red Sea. Yet, as the biblical narrative progresses, God's active involvement decreases and human actions accelerate.

In this way, God is like a parent. In a child's early years, the parent does almost everything for the child: feeding, putting to sleep, carrying. But as children get older, parents let them do more on their own. Children learn to walk and talk, and ultimately, they grow and make all of their own decisions. Now, unlike a parent, God still has the power to intervene and change the course of our lives. But the burden first falls on us to turn to God. That is the responsibility inherent in free will.

We could probe many more aspects of Jewish theology, and throughout the book, as we explore Jewish history and holidays, we will uncover other ways Jews have understood God and God's role in the world. But as a rabbi, most of the questions I am asked center around the role God plays in our lives. In particular, people come to me with confusion and frustration when they experience pain or tragedy. Why, they ask (often more with their eyes and faces than their words), do bad things to happen to good people? Does God allow these bad things to happen? If God can intervene, why does God not do so?

WHY DO BAD THINGS HAPPEN TO GOOD PEOPLE?

These are questions not just for Jews. People of all faiths struggle with them. And many profound answers have been offered. I have been enriched by conversations, for example, with Christian friends, who have shared with me their experiences of being comforted, when suffering, by recalling the sufferings of Jesus on the cross. And I think my Christian friends have also been moved by some of the answers that Jewish thinkers have offered, over the centuries, to the question, How should I think about suffering, in light of the claim that God is the genesis of all? I canvas several approaches below. But perhaps more important than any single one of the responses I canvas is the two-pronged insistence, which underpins each of these responses, that such weighty theological questions need to be pursued first with *humility*. We never know the absolute answer to God's will because *we are not God*; thus humility is a fundament of any pathway to God. The second is a sense of *faithful wrestling and struggle*, struggle befitting the heaviness and awesomeness of the task of trying to find meaning in a world filled with suffering and tragedy (in Hebrew the name *Israel* means "one who struggles with God").

With that two-pronged prelude, here are several traditional Jewish approaches to questions concerning the relationship of God and human suffering:

1. The Job Approach: The Job approach says God's ways are inscrutable. We can cry out and question, but we may never fully understand the way God works in the world.

This is the approach we find in the biblical Book of Job (named for its protagonist). When we meet Job, we see a righteous and prosperous man, blessed by God. But following a wager with a figure known as HaSatan, which in Hebrew means "the adversary," God strips Job of his family and his wealth. He is left destitute and suffering.

Job's friends tell him he must have done something to anger God. They urge him to confess. But Job is confident he has done nothing to anger God. So he continues to suffer.

And then finally Job cries out. He asks God why God has done this to him. God answers with a series of questions. The underlying message of these questions is that *God is God. And Job is not.* The questions Job asks are not questions for which he will ever have the answer. God's ways are ultimately unknowable to human beings. In the end, Job regains his prosperity and creates another family. But his questions remain unanswered.

Job is a difficult book because a person could read it and conclude God is capricious or even wicked. Why let a righteous man suffer on account of a wager with the adversary? But the Jewish sages look to Job as an example of persisting in life and faith amid the reality of suffering. We do not know why we suffer. To pretend there always is a clear explanation—as Job's friends do—is to lack humility. Rather, we do our best to live and remain committed to God when God's ways can never be fully understood and explained.

2. The Jeremiah Approach: Jeremiah is the biblical prophet who warned of the destruction of Judea by the Babylonians in the sixth century BCE and then accompanied the Israelites into exile when the Babylonians conquered them. Along with other prophets, Jeremiah said God was using the Babylonians to punish the Israelites for their lack of faithfulness and to urge them to return to their sacred ways. But Jeremiah went even further: he said God *accompanied* the Israelites into exile. Before Jeremiah, the destruction of a people meant the loss of their god. That's how empires were built. One group would conquer another. The conquered group would assimilate into the religion and culture of their victor. But Jeremiah says the God of Israel stays with the people even in exile. The Israelites, in turn, remain loyal to God, working toward their return to the land and ultimate redemption.

The broader implication of Jeremiah's prophesying is that God walks with us through tragedy and struggle. God is ever-present. During the Holocaust, a great rabbi named Kalonymus Shapira was imprisoned in the Warsaw ghetto. Other prisoners looked to him for guidance, and he led a small synagogue that met in secret. The men and women in his community constantly asked him how God could have let them become prisoners to the Nazis with women and children dying every day.

Rabbi Shapira's responses evolved, which can be traced in the diary he kept. The diary survived because as the war progressed and more of the prisoners in the ghetto were taken to death camps, the rabbi realized he would probably not survive the war. So, he placed the diary in a canister and buried it. Rabbi Shapira was murdered in 1943. A construction worker found his diary in 1945.[4]

Initially Rabbi Shapira described the war and imprisonment as a test of faith. He urged his followers to remain strong. Yet, as word of the death camps seeped into the ghetto, his writing took on a different tone. He told his followers that God was crying alongside them. He said God's tears were so powerful that if one of them were to escape from heaven to earth, it would destroy the entire world. Rabbi Shapira was echoing the Book of Jeremiah's discussion of God's tears: "Oh, that my head were a spring of water and my eyes a fountain of tears I would weep day and night for the slain of my people" (Jeremiah 9:1).

This imagery is powerful. Without denying God's omnipotence, Jeremiah's evocation of God's weeping focuses on qualities other than omnipotence: solidarity, intimacy, God made vulnerable because of God's love for God's people. When God's beloved suffer, God suffers alongside them. As Jeremiah puts it, God weeps "for the slain of my people."

3. The Maimonides Approach: Maimonides was the leading rabbi of the Middle Ages. Living in Spain and Egypt, he wrote numerous books still studied by scholars, including *The Guide to the Perplexed*. Among Jewish theologians, he is most famous for saying that we cannot say much about God because God is so much vaster than we are. We simply do not truly understand God's power and purposes. All we can do is seek to live by God's laws. In addressing the reality of human suffering, Maimonides, who also worked as a physician, integrated into his accounts of suffering his observations of human behavior and the natural world.

He theorized three categories of suffering. First, suffering flows from the fact that we are physical beings living in a physical world: to exist as physical beings means we are at risk of suffering exactly because we are part of the natural world. For example, the surface of the earth rests on tectonic plates. This structure makes life possible. At the same time, when those plates shift, earthquakes and tsunamis result. The same conditions that make life possible also make death and suffering inevitable.

The second kind of suffering comes from human behavior. We hurt and cause pain in others. We murder, steal, lie, and cheat. Human evil is not an indictment against God. It is a problem for human beings. We have free will, and that freedom permits us to cause suffering for another. Thus, asking why God didn't stop the Holocaust is a meaningless question. It is like asking why the sun doesn't shine at night. God cannot stop human beings from using the freedom we have. The Holocaust is not something God could have stopped because human beings inflicted it on one another, and God does not interfere with human freedom. Part of God's power is God's restraint and enabling of human freedom.

The third kind of suffering is that which we inflict on ourselves. Maimonides says this suffering is the most frequent by far. We hurt our health by smoking. We increase our blood pressure by working in a stressful job. We fail to trust our own desires and intuitions or we trust our desires too much. Ultimately, our own actions often cause us to suffer.

Maimonides thus credited suffering not to God, but to the natural world and to humanity itself. When suffering comes, as it inevitably will, he said we should take that suffering to God. One of the ways we bring that suffering to God is through prayer, as we will see in chapter 7.

4. The Lurianic Approach: Isaac Luria was a seventeenth-century leader in the Jewish mystical tradition. (His writings were a key inspiration to Rabbi Shapira.) The Jewish mystics searched for and focused on hidden messages and meanings within the texts of the Bible and early rabbinic writings. But they also strictly followed traditional Jewish practices. In other words, they were not a group set apart from the broader community; rather, they were often the most learned and active members of the Jewish community. In order to study Jewish mystical texts, one was supposed to have mastered the Bible and the Talmud, be married with children, and be over age forty. These requirements sought to ensure that a person who studied these powerful texts was grounded enough in family and community so as not to get lost in or overwhelmed by them.

Luria lived in the city of Sfat in Northern Israel. Sfat had become a haven for Jews who had been expelled from Spain during the fifteenth century. Before the expulsion, Spain had been a center for Jewish mystical teachings. Thus, Sfat became known for its openness to Jewish mystical tradition. The mystics in Sfat had deeply personal reasons to reflect on questions of theodicy because they lived in the shadow of the Spanish inquisition. While some of their ancestors had escaped, others had been murdered or forcibly converted. In reflecting on God's role in the world and the persistent suffering of the Jewish people, they developed a theological concept called *tzimtzum*. As we noted earlier, the Hebrew word means "contraction," and the teaching of *tzimtzum* is that when God created the world, God contracted from it. If God had not contracted, God's presence would fill the world and leave no space for human beings. God's presence and power were so vast that human beings could live only if God partially withdrew and made space for them. The suffering we see and experience is a result of this withdrawal. It is the requisite cost of human existence. But when human beings follow God's teachings and perform acts of kindness and devotion, they expand the world and make more space for God, thereby proportionately reducing the godless space that causes suffering

5. **The Kaplan Approach:** Mordecai Kaplan was a prominent modern Jewish theologian who died at age 102 in 1984. Born into a traditional Jewish family in Romania, he immigrated with his parents to America at age eight. His life spanned the monumental events of Jewish life, including the mass immigration of the late nineteenth century, the Holocaust, and the establishment of the state of Israel. Amid all of these events, Kaplan's view of God changed, and because he wrote more than twenty books, his thinking shaped many others. Kaplan totally rejects the idea of a supernatural God. Instead, he describes God as "the sum of all the animating organizing forces and relationships which are forever making a cosmos out of chaos."[5] To believe in God is, he writes, "to reckon with life's creative forces, tendencies and potentialities as forming an organic unity, and as giving meaning to life by virtue of that unity." To believe in God is to believe our life and actions serve a larger purpose. What that purpose is depends on who and where we are.

Kaplan says God is not responsible for human suffering, nor is God capable of directly relieving suffering. God is limited because God is a force, not a being with the ability to intervene in history or support someone in need. The God of the Bible is metaphor for the powerful forces that led to creative growth and civilization. But while God cannot intervene directly, God does give us the tools and strength to respond to suffering. God cannot explain or solve the loss, pain, and tragedies we face in life. Rather, God is the name we give to the forces of goodness, love, and creativity we draw from in responding to them.

One of Kaplan's most articulate and influential disciples is Rabbi Harold Kushner. He wrote several books, including the celebrated *When Bad Things Happen to Good People*. Kushner's son Aaron died at age fourteen from a rare disease called progeria, which manifests as rapid aging. Kushner's book reflected on the way he—as a man who had devoted himself to God and faith—dealt with the senseless loss of his son. Kushner wrote that God did not intervene as a supernatural force. Rather, God dwelt in friends who reached out to him, the community who supported him, the rituals that guided him back into life, and the love of others that reminded him that life is worth living. As Kushner put it, "God sends us strength and determination of which we did not believe ourselves capable, so that we can deal with, or live with, problems that no one can make go away."[6]

Kushner also emphasizes that we are not control of what happens, but we do control how we respond—and we ought to respond to the sufferings of the world by trying to mend the ills of the world and abide by God's commandments as closely as possible. Action is the answer to the question of how we respond when bad things happen to good people.

I first read Kushner twenty years ago, and one of his teachings that has always stuck with me is his observation that the Hebrew language has two words for *why*: *maduah* and *lama*. *Maduah* means "from what cause?" Let's say the lights went out. If we asked, "*Maduah* did the lights go out?" the answer could be, "Someone flipped the switch." *Lama* is different. *Lama* combines two Hebrew words *l'*, meaning "to," and *mah*, meaning "what." *Lama* means "to what end?" So to ask, "*Lama* did our lights go out?" the answer could be, "To allow us to appreciate the darkness. Perhaps to bring us closer to one another, to create a shared and memorable experience we could get through together." *Lama* orients us to the future; it seeks out the *meaning* of the event in question.

When tragedy strikes—when a loved one is diagnosed with cancer, when a car wreck disables a friend—and we turn to God, we gain no comfort when we ask *maduah*, what caused God to do this. That's imagining a God in which we don't believe. That's seeing God as one who flips a light switch and someone dies. Instead we ask God *lama*, why, to what end? What is the meaning of the terrible event—and how can I and my community actively seek and concoct that meaning? How can we shape what happened? We can decide that the purpose of a tragedy is to make us miserable or to punish us for something we did. Or we can decide the purpose is to call out the best within us. There is no objective right answer. The true answer is the one we give with our lives.

Where is God in all this? God's presence is found in our

choice. When we choose to bring comfort to the mourning, when we choose to love, when we choose to lift up the poor and do the right thing when the wrong thing is easier and cheaper, God becomes real. God's hands become our hands, and our loves become the loves of God.

CONCLUSION

In this chapter, we have gotten just a taste of Jewish thinking about God. The ideas we've reviewed in the last few pages suggest the range of beliefs within the Jewish community. Judaism has never wholly embraced a systematic theology, in part because Judaism began as a family—the children of Abraham—rather than a set of beliefs and practices. Just as a family embraces and includes members with different points of view, so has the Jewish community lived together with different conceptions of God. Recall Rabbi Karff's wisdom: "Life is not a puzzle to solve but a mystery to embrace."[7]

But for all their differences, each of the Jewish conceptions of God is responsive to the same set of sacred texts—the voluble and varied sacred Scriptures that animate Jewish prayer and theologies. We turn to that canon of texts in the next chapter.

~~~~~~~~~~~~~~~~

2

TEXTS

~~~~~~~~~~~~~~~~

I have an annoying habit that occasionally gets in the way of good conversation. Whenever I visit someone's home or apartment, I immediately gravitate to their bookshelves. I start looking at them and can't take my eyes away. Sometimes minutes pass, and it feels like seconds to me. A few times people have commented that I should abandon the books and join in the conversation. But books feel sacred to me. They are like a treasure I need to explore and uncover.

What is it about books that evoke our reverence? Why do Jews take pride in being known as the people of the Book? We believe our sacred book comes from God. God revealed it to Moses atop Mount Sinai. According to one midrash (rabbinic legend), God—the God who showed up to Moses as flame—revealed the Torah to Moses with black fire written on white fire to symbolize the holiness and power of its words. Not all books are made of fire, but all of them seem to partake of a kind of magic.

Texts draw us in because they reveal the stories we tell about ourselves. They remind us who we are and how we aim to live.

The text at the center of Judaism is the Hebrew Bible. It is also known as the Jewish Bible and the Hebrew Scriptures—and, with the books reordered a bit, the same text is known to Christians as the Old Testament. Perhaps the most accurate name is TaNaK, which is an acronym capturing the three major sections of the Hebrew Bible. These are

Torah, which are the five books of Moses (Genesis, Exodus, Leviticus, Numbers, and Deuteronomy); *Neviim,* which are the prophetic books like Amos and Jeremiah; and *Ketuvim,* the Writings, which include First Kings, Second Kings, the Books of Psalms, Esther, and others. Of these three sections, Torah is the most important. Jews read the Torah, the five books of Moses, from beginning to end in synagogue every year. Sections from the other parts of the TaNaK are also read each year. In many synagogues, the reading of the Torah is the focal point of a prayer service. The sermon usually revolves around the verses read from it.

The TaNaK is not, however, our only sacred text. The other is the Talmud, which is sixty-six volumes of rabbinic debates on and discussions of law, belief, and wisdom. The Talmud began as a series of conversations that were eventually committed to memory and written down around the sixth century CE. When speaking to Christian groups, I often describe the Talmud as the "Jewish New Testament." This is an imperfect analogy because the Talmud does not have quite the same status in Judaism as the New Testament does in Christianity. But the analogy is helpful because it underlines that Jews and Christians share the TaNaK/Old Testament, but that each community responds to that shared scripture with a different textual deposit: Jews respond with the Talmud and Christians respond with the New Testament. And the analogy is helpful because from a historical perspective, the Talmud emerged around the same time that early Christians were writing the texts that would become the New Testament.

Both the New Testament and the Talmud reflect a new religious reality in the first century CE. The temple—God's dwelling place on earth, situated in the center of Jerusalem—is in peril. It is filled with corruption and threatened constantly by the ruling Roman empire. Finally, after a series of wars between 66 and 70 CE, the temple is destroyed. How will God's people survive?

For Christians, following the way of Jesus became the path to God. Jesus was the New Temple. Jesus atoned for the sins of the people. Jesus's message found expression in the New Testament. A new religion soon emerged.

For Jews, following the teachings of the Talmud became the path to God. The authors of the Talmud saw themselves as the spiritual descendants of Moses and the Prophets. They both preserved and evolved Judaism for a new era.

While the Talmud is second in status only to the TaNaK, other sacred texts also shaped Jewish self-understanding. They include commentaries written by highly respected rabbis of the Middle Ages as well as books of philosophy and law by the twelfth-century scholar Moses Maimonides. Each of these books is studied with intensity because study is a form of worship. Understanding how Jews engage and study texts reveals basic Jewish values and truths. As one great rabbi said, "When I pray I talk to God. When I study God talks to me."[1] How do we hear God talking to us today? Why is study so important from a spiritual perspective? Why has study helped define what it means to be Jewish? What truths and insights can Jewish methods of study offer people of all faiths?

TORAH LISHMA AND TEXTS FOR LIVING

At its core, Jews study texts for no other reason than to study them: as Albert Einstein put it, "The pursuit of knowledge for its own sake, an almost fanatical love of justice, and the desire for personal independence —these are the features of the Jewish tradition which make me thank my lucky stars that I belong to it."[2]

Einstein's phrase—the pursuit of knowledge for its own sake—echoes a two thousand-year-old Jewish ideal known as Torah Lishmah, or learning for its own sake. In other words, we don't learn to pass tests or even master a new skill. We learn because that's what God created us to do. We learn because of the intrinsic value of learning itself.

Yet at the same time, Jews recognize that when we study sacred texts, we are given a picture of how we ought to live. Torah and Talmud guide us in living meaningful lives. We need such a guide because we are, to paraphrase Socrates, meaning-seeking animals. When we study, we learn how to build meaning into our relationships, our actions, our prayers.

Einstein also offers us a second doorway into Jewish learning. His theory of relativity—that matter is always in motion and we cannot understand the world from an absolute point of view—mirrors the way Jews understand the meaning of texts. One of Einstein's biographers, Steven Gimbel, saw this connection. He wrote, "The heart of the Talmudic view is that there is an absolute truth, but this truth is not directly and completely available to us. It turns out that exactly the same style of thinking occurs in the relativity theory and in some of Einstein's other research."[3] The key phrase here is "not directly and completely available to us." Study is a process of discerning and uncovering God's truth in God's word. It takes continual application of our minds and our hearts, and it is never fully complete.

This approach may upset those of us who yearn for a quick and easy path to truth. And, in some ways, each of us always yearns for that. Life is complicated, and we wish we had a place where we could always find all the answers we need. In some areas of life, we do. We do not murder or steal or commit other clearly forbidden acts. When a loved one dies, we have a clear process for mourning and remembering. But God's Word is too rich to yield instant understanding of all of life's mysteries. That takes study. And it is in the studied pursuit of truth that we find meaning and our purpose for living.

COMMENTARY

The Jewish library includes many commentaries on the Torah and Talmud (just as the larger Christian library might include Augustine's commentary on the Psalms or Calvin's commentaries on the Prophets). The commentaries were written by the most respected rabbis of different eras of Jewish history. There were commentaries on the Torah, the Talmud, and even commentaries on the commentaries. The goal of the commentaries was to figure the intent, meaning, and application of the texts in their time and place. Certain commentaries gained prominence because they were written by especially notable authors or because the commentary struck readers as especially profound. Commentary was an ancient form of what happens on social media today. On Facebook, a post that gains many likes will usually be highlighted and given more prominence. Similarly, a rabbinical writing cited by others would gain prominence and eventually be written down and passed on to future generations. Thus, if you walk into a Jewish school and see students studying from an open book, the voices on the page may range from the first century to the nineteenth century.

The ability to knit together commentaries on commentaries has expanded with the advent of the internet. There is now a Jewish website founded by early employees of Google that seeks to gather all the most cited Jewish texts and then hyperlink to new commentaries written by modern rabbis and scholars. The potential for new insights is virtually endless.

Jewish study is guided by a metaphorical framework known as PARDES, which is a Hebrew word meaning "orchard." It is also an acronym for the words *Peshat, Remez, Drash*, and *Sod*. Each of these is an approach to studying text. They are undergirded by the principle that God is still speaking to us.

The first approach—peshat—is the most widely used. If someone asks you for the peshat of the text, he or she is asking for your best understanding of the literal meaning of the biblical verse. Hebrew words often have multiple meanings. The peshat is the sages' understanding of the particular meaning of the word as used in a biblical verse. The second approach—remez—refers to the allegorical meaning of the verse. The Hebrew word *remez* means "hint." When we look for the remez meaning, we are looking for hints of another message within a particular word or verse. Drash is an application of the word or verse for our lives. It is sometimes called the homiletical interpretation. The drash is what a preacher or rabbi might say the verse teaches us. The final level is sod. The word *sod* means "secret." Sod refers to the hidden meaning of a verse. The sod interpretation often seems to have little connection to the verse itself. It can come from one rabbi's association with a particular letter in one of the words in the verse. More often, it feels like a riddle within which is hidden some core truth about the world.

Let's see the way the PARDES method works through an examination of an enigmatic biblical story: Jacob's dream of a ladder reaching from heaven to earth in Genesis 28:12: "He [Jacob] had a vision in a dream. A ladder was standing on the ground, its top reaching up toward heaven as Divine angels were going up and down on it" (author's translation). The key word is *ladder*. In Hebrew the word used is *sulam*. Translating the word as "ladder" requires a peshat interpretation because no scholar is certain the word *sulam* necessarily means ladder! The word *sulam* is not found anywhere else in the Bible, and at Mount Sinai, God did not reveal a Hebrew-English dictionary. Therefore, scholars have no context in which they can see how the word is used. But ladder seems to be the likely meaning in the context of the story. Thus, the translation of sulam as "ladder" is a peshat interpretation.

The next level of interpretation is remez. What else might the word *sulam* mean? A ladder fulfills a certain function. It bridges heights. What else bridges heights? A spiral does. Thus, from a remez interpretation, the word *sulam* might refer to a spiraling staircase or ramp bridging heaven and earth. Spirals have sacred significance in many cultures, including those of the ancient Near East. Spirals are found throughout the natural world, and they frequently symbolize growth. The old dies away as the new comes forward.

This interpretation makes sense because Jacob's dream happens at a pivotal point in his life. Like his grandfather Abraham, he is leaving behind his homeland and his father's house on a journey to a new home. His relationship with God is also changing. He now has the blessing of the firstborn son. The covenant Abraham made with God will pass through him. The spiral may symbolize the spiritual journey God has prepared for him.

There is no way to prove one interpretation is the right one. Different perspectives can coexist. You might be thinking this openness to a variety of interpretations leads to chaos. How can we ever know the truth? Well, the Jewish sages distinguished between two genres in their sacred writings. They are *halakhah*, law, and *agaddah*, legend. *Halakhic* questions—legal questions—have a right answer: there is one proper blessing we say before eating bread, and even if the rabbis had to debate what exactly should be said in that blessing, they eventually arrived at a decision that is followed by everybody.

By contrast, when considering agaddah legends, you need not be on the lookout for a single right answer. Different interpretations coexist. Agaddah allows for creativity and subjective insight. We understand God's Word differently based on our life experience and intelligence. Think of it this way: If you see a movie with a friend, you may leave with different interpretations and perspectives on the movie. But you would agree that you saw the same movie and paid the same ticket price. The name of the film and the price are like halakhah. The reviews you give it are the agaddah.

In Judaism, God's Word speaks to us as we are, and there is no objective way to interpret stories. There is an objective way to act. We cannot subjectively decide that to murder or steal is OK. But using our intelligence, creativity, and other intellectual tools, we can seek to derive subjective interpretations of biblical stories. Jacob's ladder is one of them.

The next level of interpretation is drash. Drash offers an interpretation of a biblical text that leads to an application in our lives. A drash for Jacob's ladder is that it symbolizes Mount Sinai, connecting heaven and earth. Mount Sinai is the site where God revealed the Torah to the Jewish people. The Torah is a way of bringing human beings closer to heaven. Its laws and teachings teach us how to walk in God's ways. Jacob's dream symbolizes this truth. It reminds us that Torah is the bridge between heaven and earth. Torah is where heaven and earth touch. This drash interpretation reminds us why we follow the laws of Torah. They lead us to God.

The sod interpretation of Jacob's ladder is that the ladder symbolizes Jacob himself. His head is in heaven, dreaming of the world as it ought to be. In his dream, he sees the world from God's point of view. But his feet are resting on earth, in the world as it is. His life is the bridge between the two. Jacob's dream reveals what it means to be created in the image of God. Human beings bridge heaven and earth. Our soul rests in God, while our physical bodies are grounded here on life. Our purpose is to bridge these two worlds through living a life of faith.

This four-pronged approach to reading a text—peshat, remez, drash, sod—may strike you as strange. Isn't the Bible simply the Word of God that we can learn and understand? Why do we need all of these different approaches? Is God trying to confuse us? No. From the Jewish perspective, God's Word is so rich and profound that we need to look at it from different perspectives in order to understand and apply it fully. Think of a memorable work of art. Part of what makes it beautiful is that we can look at it from different perspectives. We see different things in it. What I see in a still-life painting may differ from what an art historian sees or what an architect sees or what a fruit grower sees. Great works of art evoke different insightful responses. The Bible is more than a great work of art. It is a book capturing eternal truths. The different perspectives we bring illuminate that truth in ways meaningful and applicable for every person in every era.

My Journey to a Life of Faith

Study has been an essential way to God for me for as long as I remember. From first to fifth grades I attended a Jewish day school. My going there was a bit of a fluke because my mom was a public school teacher, and I began first grade at a local public school. But about a week into the year, my mom pulled me out because she found me after school standing against a chalkboard with my nose in a circle, and no teacher was anywhere in the room. It turned out the teacher had punished me for not bringing a pencil to class and then disappeared while making me stand against the chalkboard. My mom was furious. The only school that would take me after the year had started was the school that had opened up in my family's synagogue the year before.

Jewish day schools are not nearly as prevalent as Catholic schools, and they are especially rare in Reform synagogues like the one to which my family belonged, primarily because Jewish immigrants had typically seen public school as part of the process of becoming American. Nevertheless, our rabbi had been determined to start one because he believed only an educated Jewish community could survive in America.

Fortunately, the school accepted me, and on the day I arrived, they welcomed me with a special ritual. The principal gave me a copy of the Hebrew Bible, opened it to the first page, and then placed a small bowl of honey with a spoon and sliced apples next to me. She asked me to take a dab of honey and place it in my mouth. Then I was to open my Bible and start reading the opening words aloud. I did so. Then I was to enjoy the apples and honey and keep reading.

The goal of the ritual is to create an association between sweetness and learning. Studying God's Word is an expression of love and joy. This ritual has been practiced for hundreds of years; some teachers even place honey on the page itself, though I suspect that might make the book difficult to use.

In any case, my experience at the Jewish day school ignited a love of learning. Studying the Bible felt like exploring my family's history and adventures, along with discovering the life lessons and practices derived from those experiences. Even the ways I learned to refer to the biblical characters themselves demonstrated the familial connection. I learned not to just say Abraham. We say Avraham Avinu, which means "Abraham our father." And Moses is Moshe Rabenu, which means "Moses our rabbi." These figures are living, breathing members of the family. When we study their words, we, in a mystical way, bring them back to life.

Our family lives on for eternity. And we breathe life into them when we study the words they left us.

Even though attending a Jewish elementary school ignited a love of study, I fell away from Torah study in middle school and high school. We'd moved from Houston to Milwaukee, where the public schools were excellent. Debate, sports, and the school newspaper took up my extra time. My faith was strong, but I put little effort into growing and studying it. Everything else took priority.

I returned to serious Jewish study in college. This timing is somewhat ironic because college is usually a time when people fall away from childhood religion. But college can also be a time of growth, and we can grow into our past rather than away from it. It was in college that I learned a Hebrew word embodying this idea. The word is *teshuvah*. Sometimes it is translated as "repentance," but the literal meaning is "return." Teshuvah is a return to our best selves.

In contrast to Christianity, Judaism does not have an idea of original sin. We are not tainted by Adam and Eve's original disobedience. While they occasionally argued about human nature, the Jewish sages generally held that our soul yearns to do good. We are often pulled away from that yearning. Our baser instincts influence us, or we are corrupted by the wider society. But one of the core Hebrew prayers said by traditional Jews every day thanks God for the "pure soul You have given me." This positive view of human potential leads to the concept of teshuvah, of return, to our original highest selves.

For me that return began with a college job. I loved the campus at Stanford University, but it often felt like a bubble, and I wanted a pursuit to take me occasionally off campus.

Since I knew Hebrew from my childhood school, I made an appointment at a local synagogue and asked if I could help teach Sunday school and tutor kids preparing for bar or bat mitzvah (the Jewish coming of age ceremony, at which many kids read from the Torah in public for the first time). The rabbi, surprisingly, said no. "Rather," he said, "I'd like you to teach Bible to our high school students." I wanted a job and, for better or worse, have never lacked confidence in my ability to take on a new challenge! So I taught the class. It went well, and the students asked me to continue the next year with a class on Talmud. Even though I had little experience studying Talmud—let alone teaching it—I agreed.

Something happened to me in teaching those classes. The texts felt relevant in a way I never imagined they could. They awakened in me a recognition of something I was missing. I realized I was seeking a calling, a purpose, a way of living a meaningful life. The texts I studied in my college classes educated me. They helped me learn to think critically. But they did not challenge and inspire me in the same way the biblical and Talmudic texts did. My college reading list was about the facts of life. My Jewish text list was about the *meaning* of life.

HOW STUDY SUSTAINED JUDAISM

Those texts did not just help me discern a new path for my life. They also showed me the way the Jewish people had held on to life for thousands of years. In chapter 4, we will discuss the centrality of the land of Israel to the Jewish people. It is our homeland and spiritual center. Yet, until 1948, there was no state of Israel, and Judaism survived and thrived. If America did not exist as a country for two thousand years, would we still have people identifying as Americans and referring to it as their homeland? Probably not. And even today, more Jews reside outside Israel than inside of it.

Something else held Jews together over the centuries. It was the text, God's Word. Seeking to capture this idea, the nineteenth-century poet Heinrich Heine described the Torah as the Jews' "portable homeland." Wherever Jews went, the text went with them, and so long as they had and studied the text, they remained God's people.

We continue to read and study God's words in synagogues and churches every day. Those words range from the poetry of the Psalms to the debates of the Talmud to the literary insights of the rabbinic commentaries to the foundational narratives of Genesis. We believe God's Word remains eternally timely, and it is through God's Word that we make sense of the world. The Bible is not a piece of literature whose message is confined to a particular time and place. It reveals truth and offers guidance for every generation. To receive those truths and guidance, we have to study it. A text-based religion creates an ongoing engagement with God and a community of study. Like a physical homeland, a sacred text ties together past, present, and future.

The sacred texts of Judaism also allowed belief in one God to spread around the world. In the ancient Near East, gods were associated with particular locales. The Jebusite god, for example, reigned in Jebusite territory. Shrines in that territory allowed people to access and make sacrifices to that god. If the Jebusites were conquered, their god was assimilated into the god of the conquering tribe.

The Hebrew Bible revolted against this idea. God speaks to Abraham, and God's first words are "Journey from your homeland, from your father's house to the land that I will show you" (Genesis 12:1, author's translation). Judaism begins in a journey from one location toward another. And Judaism begins outside of the Promised Land in order to teach that God is accessible everywhere. To be sure, certain places let us feel closer to God. For the ancient Israelites, the temple in Jerusalem was a place where we offered sacrifices in order to feel closer to God. But God did not dwell in the temple alone. King Solomon's prayer at the dedication of that temple made that clear when he said, "But will God really dwell on earth? The heavens, even the highest heaven, cannot contain you. How much less this temple I have built!" (1 Kings 8:27).

ONE GOD, MANY CONVERSATIONS

The text not only speaks to each of us directly when we read and study it; it also allows for a multigenerational conversation. We hear from our ancestors whenever we study ancient commentaries on the biblical text. We also speak to our descendants when we offer our own responses to and interpretations of it.

Picture your own reading of the Bible: If you are Christian and reading the Gospels, you hear Jesus's words. You even hear the words of the Old Testament as he quotes them. You have your own reactions to the text, and either note them to yourself or write them in the margins or in a journal. This is an ongoing conversation with God's words. You may even recall a preacher's words or a book you read that commented on the text you are reading. You may note those recollections as well. The notion of experiencing and receiving instruction from God through the text begins in Judaism. God spoke to Abraham, and Abraham began a conversation with God. That conversation continues today. And each of our voices matters because they add to it. We join a sacred conversation begun long before we were born, and which will continue long after we are gone.

~~~~~~~~~~

3

ELECTION, OR
GOD'S JEDI
MASTERS

~~~~~~~~~~

Whenever I speak at churches, I am asked when I was *called* to be a rabbi. The question surprised me at first because Jews tend not to use that particular phrasing when describing the decision to become a member of the clergy. In synagogues, for example, I am usually asked when I *decided* to be a rabbi. What's the difference? The first phrasing of the question emphasizes the agency of God. God *calls* a person to the clergy. The other phrasing emphasizes the agency of human beings. We *choose* to enter the clergy.

The more I encountered and answered these questions, however, the more I began to see calling and choosing as complementary rather than contradictory locutions. We can be *called* to something. But that call is meaningless if we *choose* not to answer. We can choose to ignore it. We can choose to pretend we did not hear it. We can choose to believe it was intended for someone else. The answer we give to a call is as consequential as the call itself. Similarly, we can choose something, but if that choice is not consistent with the best vision God has for our lives, it will come to nothing.

This recognition helped illuminate my own vocational path, but it also helped me understand one of the most challenging themes in Judaism: the idea that Jews are God's chosen people. To be chosen is to be called. But this understanding leads to further questions. Who does the calling? Why are the Jews called? And what are the Jewish people called to do? Have the Jews answered the call?

This chapter looks at different answers to these questions. We will also see the way the idea of chosen people has been used and abused throughout history, and the ways it continues to shape Jewish self-understanding, Christianity, and even the United States of America.

BIBLICAL CALLING

The first question—Who does the calling?—is the easiest to answer. God does the calling. But the Jewish people are not the first ones called. The Bible begins with Adam and Eve. They are the parents of—and symbol of—all humanity. They are called to live in the garden of Eden and not eat from the Tree of Knowledge. They fail. Subsequent generations also fall into wickedness. Then God calls Noah to preserve a remnant of humanity after God destroys the world in a massive flood. Initially, Noah succeeds. He answers the call by building an ark and riding out the flood with his family and representatives of each of the animal species. But Noah's mission ends in failure after he falls into drunkenness. Noah saved himself, but he did not fulfill God's hope that he would be a blessing to humanity. That mission—to be a blessing to the world—is what distinguishes God's call to Abraham. In the verses announcing God's call to Abraham, God says, "I will bless those who bless you, and whoever curses you I will curse; and all peoples on earth will be blessed through you" (Genesis 12:3). God calls Abraham not only to follow a unique set of laws. God calls on Abraham to be a blessing to the nations of the world.

We will probe what it means to be a blessing to the world later in this chapter, but the story of God choosing Abraham leaves us with a lingering question. Why did God choose Abraham in particular? The Bible does not suggest Abraham had any special qualities or achievements. It seems God simply calls him out of the blue. The Jewish sages, however, seek to fill in Abraham's backstory and explain what led God to choose him. They draw from midrash—Jewish legends use to figure out the meaning of biblical texts—in doing so. (Midrash is a variation on the word *drash*, homiletical interpretation, which we met in the last chapter.)

WHY ABRAHAM?

This midrash imagines Abraham as a boy. During Abraham's life, groups in the Near East believed in multiple competing and localized gods. Those gods were represented with idols. Abraham's father was an idol maker. One day he left the teenage Abram (God changes his name to Abraham after his circumcision) alone in the store. An older well-respected man in the community came in to purchase an idol. Abram then asked him, "Why would you worship a statue we just made yesterday?" The man left without buying it.

Abram realized that these human-made idols had no power. The next day, while his father was out again, he destroyed all of them. Even though his father was distraught, God was impressed with Abram's insight and commitment. God then chose him to begin a new tribe dedicated to belief in and the practices of the one true God.

This legend shows us that the Jewish sages want to emphasize the ways Abraham challenged the conventions of his time. The world of the ancient Near East was filled with tribal conflict, and Abram understood that this was not the kind of world God envisioned. God gave human beings free will, but God did not expect them to use their free will to destroy one another. The generations of Adam and Eve and of Noah did not succeed in elevating human morality. Rather, they illustrated its destructive potential. God gives humanity another opportunity with Abraham because Abraham sensed the distance between the world as it is and the world as it ought to be. He realized there was a problem. So God called him to do something about it. In other words, God chose Abraham to steer humanity on a new course. And all the nations of the world will eventually be blessed through him.

RESPONSIBILITIES

What was Abraham called to do? What responsibilities does being chosen by God entail in Judaism? The best way to understand the way Jews have traditionally answered these questions is to use the example of a marriage. A marriage is a relationship in which two people choose each other. That choice results in both concrete and more abstract responsibilities. Concretely, they need to care for each other, remain faithful to each other, raise children together, and so on. More abstractly, they need to love each other, respect each other, and accept each other.

Similarly, the relationship between God and the Jewish people entails the Jewish people affirming certain abstract beliefs (chief among them that one God created the world and revealed the way to live in a book known as the Torah) and accepting particular responsibilities. Indeed, the responsibilities inherent in the relationship fall upon both God and the Jewish people.

As part of their covenantal relationship, God promises Abraham two things. The first is land. The Jewish people will dwell and possess the land of Israel. They will live on that land for all time. The second promise is descendants. Abraham's descendants will be as numerous as the stars in the sky and sand on the shore.

In exchange for land and descendants, Abraham agrees to follow God's commandments. Abraham also agrees to teach his descendants God's ways. As Genesis 18:19 puts it, "For I have chosen him, so that he will direct his children and his household after him to keep the way of the LORD by doing what is right and just, so that the LORD will bring about for Abraham what he has promised him." Abraham must teach his children "what is right and just."

This phrase lacks a clear explanation in the text itself. But the Jewish sages discerned its meaning from other biblical references. The clearest and most relevant reference is in Genesis 18. God plans to destroy the cities of Sodom and Gomorrah on account of their wickedness. But God decides to see what Abraham thinks of this decision. We get a stunning glimpse of God's internal monologue in verse 17 when God says, "Shall I hide from Abraham what I am about to do? . . . For I have chosen him, so that he will direct his children and his household after him to keep the way of God by doing what is right and just."

After this monologue, what does Abraham do? He asks God if God truly wants to destroy Sodom and Gomorrah and sweep away the innocent along with the guilty. Specifically, Abraham asks God to reconsider the choice to destroy the cities if at least ten innocent people can be found. Abraham urges God to protect the innocent even as God punishes the guilty. Abraham's behavior may not seem revolutionary to us today because we live in a world where we seek to apply laws equally and rationally. Our society is imperfect, but the principle of equal justice under law and the concept of innocent until proven guilty hold sway in our culture. It was, however, revolutionary at the time. The gods of the ancient Near East prized power. Powerful kings were semi-deities themselves. Righteousness and morality were not central concerns. But for the Bible they were. And for Abraham they were. The God who speaks to Abraham changes the paradigm of what it means to be chosen by God. Power is not the sign of God's chosenness. Moral behavior is, and Abraham exemplifies it.

CHOSENNESS AND MORALITY

How do we determine what is right and just today? Even on issues about which we feel complete certainty we know that others whom we respect feel differently. Issues like immigration rights and the death penalty, for example, evoke complex and contradictory moral responses from equally spiritual and well-intentioned people.

When it comes to doing what is right and just, two general and relevant principles emerge from Jewish tradition. The first is moderation—avoiding the extremes. The meaning of moderation is articulated most clearly by Maimonides, whom we met in chapter 1. Maimonides was a physician and a scientist. He analyzed human virtues in a quasi-mathematical way. Every human characteristic, he taught, has two extremes and a mean. Most of us fall toward one of the extremes. But the path of God is the mean, the middle.

For example, consider the value of generosity or charity. The Bible includes the obligation to tithe—that is, to give 10 percent of our income to charity. In biblical times, the tithe went to the temple authorities. Today, in many Christian communities, the tithe goes to the local church. Some Jews who tithe may give to the synagogue, and other Jews may give some or all of their tithe to communal support funds. Tithing reflects the moral principle of generosity and helping those in need.

Yet, Jewish law prohibits giving away more than 20 percent of one's income. So, while tithing entails giving a minimum of 10 percent of income, it cannot exceed 20 percent. The principle is moderation. We should not give away so much that we ignore our own needs. And, we should not mistake excessive giving with righteousness because giving can easily become a form of self-righteousness. Every value can be taken to excess, and Abraham and his descendants are called to embody moderation of character.

Another illustration of this kind of moderation is found in the laws of mourning. When a loved one dies, our mourning unfolds in stages. The first is the most intense. We bury the deceased as quickly as possible. We then mourn at home for seven days with mirrors covered, surrounded by fellow mourners. After those seven days, we can return to work, but we are to avoid large social gatherings and celebrations. Only after thirty days are we permitted to visit the grave. Why? Because going back to the grave frequently in those first raw days of mourning can lead us to focus too much on death. The process of mourning is meant to honor the deceased and guide us back into life. Mourning, like other human pursuits, can be taken to excess, and God instructs Abraham and his descendants on the proper way of mourning in moderation.

This emphasis on moderation seems like a critical religious value today. We live in an age when religion and religious people are often associated with extremism. Recent studies found that when people hear the phrase "very religious," they generally think of someone who sees the world in black and white.[1] Yet, God's choice of Abraham suggests real piety is found in moderation. And moderation ultimately rests in humility. We are not God. We do not see as God sees, and extremism rests on assuredness of absolute knowledge. One knows with certainty what one must do. Moderation acknowledges we might be wrong even as we attempt to follow God's will.

SUFFERING

The second element of doing is right and just is less uplifting than the first. It is the recognition that righteousness involves suffering. Being chosen does not mean being protected at all times. Rather, chosenness can expose one to hatred and violence. The Talmud views the suffering of the righteous as "pangs of love" (in Hebrew, *yissurim shel ahavah*).[2] As God says to Abraham in Genesis 15:13, "Know for certain that for four hundred years your descendants will be strangers in a country not their own and that they will be enslaved and mistreated there." Knowing this future—knowing his descendants will suffer—Abraham remains committed to the covenant with God. This verse has helped guide Jews through thousands of years of persecution. They were suffering for a purpose. They were chosen to embody God's message in the world.

Why would God desire the chosen people to suffer? Christianity answers this question by seeing Jesus's suffering as atoning for the sins of humanity. For Jews, suffering had a similar but not identical purpose. Israel suffers on behalf of humanity in order to draw humanity closer to God. Suffering is not atonement. It is service. Israel is like the frontline soldier who takes the gunshots and pushes through so that those behind him can push through as well.

Isaiah 55, which is an elaboration on God's original promise to Abraham that his people would be the ones through whom all the world is blessed, hints at this purpose. Isaiah describes the means by which Israel would bring these blessings. They would serve as a "witness to the nations" (Isaiah 55:4). In other words, Jews serve as witnesses for God, seeing the behavior of the actions and trying to model what God desires.

Being a witness is not easy. Often you have to say uncomfortable truths and suffer for your testimony. Just think of potential witnesses in trials who refuse to testify, or those who testify and are murdered as a result. Being a witness for God in a world where so many reject God is not easy. But the task serves humanity. It reveals a faith and way of life that the nations of the world will eventually embrace.

A NEW WAY OF UNDERSTANDING CHOSENNESS

This understanding of chosenness persisted through the Middle Ages, and even into modernity. Jews found meaning in suffering because they were God's witnesses on earth. Their survival amid such suffering itself was miraculous, testifying to the ultimate arrival of God's truth on earth. This self-understanding underwent a partial change in the early nineteenth century because, for the first time in hundreds of years, Jews were not forced to live in isolated ghettos in Europe. The French Revolution and the Napoleonic wars that followed led to new laws permitting Jews to interact more broadly with the overall community. They attended secular universities. They entered professions from which they had once been excluded. Some converted to Christianity. But others sought a new way to accommodate living as a Jew in a predominantly non-Jewish world. Out of this new social and political situation arose a new understanding of chosenness.

This new understanding of chosenness argued that God did not choose the Jewish people to suffer for God's sake. Rather, God chose the Jews to spread the truths of ethical monotheism—the belief in one God whom we serve through ethical behavior—to the world. Jews have this sacred mission, and they must survive as Jews in order to achieve it.

A 1937 rabbinic declaration put it this way: "Throughout the ages it has been Israel's mission to witness to the Divine in the face of every form of paganism and materialism. We regard it as our historic task to cooperate with all men in the establishment of the kingdom of God, of universal brotherhood, Justice, truth and peace on earth."[3] In other words, Jews serve as an eternal witness for God in the pursuit of moral and ethical ideals.

While this understanding of chosenness persisted among many Jews through the mid-twentieth century, it began to fade in the 1970s and 1980s; I suspect the reasons are both political and social. Many Jews disagree on the best way to achieve freedom and peace: pacifism or intervention? more government or less government? The possibility of "universal brotherhood" and "peace on earth" seemed far-fetched after the horrors of the Holocaust. Rather than naively pursue an impossible dream, Jews should focus on self-defense and building up the Jewish homeland of Israel. Discussion of Jews' universal mission virtually disappeared from rabbinic writing and sermons.

Another problem with the theology that Jews are chosen for a universal ethical mission is that one does not need to be Jewish to be a beacon of light. We all know righteous and ethical people of different religions or of no religion at all. Judaism may be a guide to an ethical life, but so are other faiths. To say Judaism has the best path to such ideals seems both improvable and ethnocentric. The missional understanding of chosenness may have worked in an era when Jews still felt separate from the larger society because of the persistence of social anti-Semitism. It gave a justification for Jews remaining different that did not depend on strict observance of Jewish law or the suffering that came from being religiously different. Yet, my own experience as a congregational rabbi suggests most Jews do not feel as if they have a uniquely special mission to teach the world the perfect moral and ethical ideal. That truth brings us to our final question:

DO JEWS STILL FEEL CHOSEN TODAY?

At a recent speaking engagement at a synagogue, I asked fifteen people I did not know whether they believed Jews are the chosen people. My exact phrasing was, "I have a question. Just answer yes or no. Do you feel Jews are the chosen people?" Fourteen out of fifteen said no. I was shocked. One of my college professors wrote an entire book explaining why the feeling of being chosen allowed American Jews to resist assimilation into America.[4] American Jews could have easily given up their Judaism; that, perhaps, would have opened up jobs and neighborhoods, which through the 1960s excluded Jews. Yet, by and large, American Jews remained Jewish. My professor argues that the lingering of belief in being chosen by God and given a special responsibility to embody spiritual and ethical truth kept Jews Jewish. Could all those feelings of being chosen have dissipated so much by 2018, the year I took my anecdotal survey? That seemed to be the case.

Yet, as a rabbi working in the trenches of Jewish community, I know most Jews have not given up on the feeling of being chosen. It still resonates in their self-understanding, but being chosen has a different meaning for today's Jews than it did for my parents and grandparents. To be chosen today does not mean to be responsible for following Jewish laws. It does not mean to embody a particular set of ethical ideals, though those remain a critical part of Jewish self-understanding. It does not mean thinking of one's self as a beacon of light. Rather, to be chosen means one is obligated to survive as a Jew. To be chosen is to be commanded to remain Jewish.

The first theologian to articulate this idea was a German-Israeli rabbi named Emil Fackenheim. He wrote in the wake of the Holocaust, and he said the experience of the Holocaust revealed a new commandment for Jews today. This commandment is "Thou Shalt Not Give Hitler a Posthumous Victory." Hitler intended to murder the world's Jews. He wanted to rid the world of Judaism. He came dangerously close to meeting his goal. Every Jew, said Fackenheim, now has an obligation to remain Jewish to ensure that never happens.[5]

This Jewish self-understanding—the feeling that one has an obligation to remain Jewish after the Holocaust—resonates for many Jews today. And this idea differs significantly from the biblical understanding of being the chosen people. In the Bible God chooses the Jewish people. Jews choose to fulfill their responsibility to God on earth.

From Fackenheim's perspective, it is not God who chooses the Jews. History does. Or, to be more precise, the events of history create a context in which Jews feel an obligation to their ancestors. Their ancestors remained Jewish. They passed on that heritage to their children. Now it is their responsibility to remain Jewish. They were chosen by birth.

Fackenheim's idea challenges me as an American deeply committed to the ideals of freedom because it suggests we have no real choice about our religion: we are bound to it by birth and by the hatred of others. We must live as Jews because we owe it to those who came before us and because of the hatred of other peoples. While I do not agree with Fackenheim's theology, I think he captures a historical reality. For most of our history, Jews did not have the choice to not identify as Jews. Part of the gift of America and the twenty-first century is that Jews have more choices than ever before. And as Fackenheim shows us, this freedom creates its own challenges because the Jewish people cannot survive if people choose not to remain Jewish.

ARGUING WITH GOD

There is one other implication of the Jewish self-understanding as God's chosen people. Jews became comfortable arguing with God. Their arguments with God are not of the vicious kind. Jewish argument with God is more like spouses arguing with one another, knowing that the argument will not destroy the relationship at its core.

Over time Jews developed certain religious attitudes that remain part of Judaism today. The word that best describes those attitudes is *chutzpah*. The word *chutzpah* comes from Yiddish, which is a combination of German and Hebrew spoken by Jews in Eastern Europe for hundreds of years. *Chutzpah* means "gall"; it typically describes risky actions that break conventional norms. Those actions tend to evoke a mixture of admiration and surprise.

We see a classic example of Jewish *chutzpah* in the musical *Fiddler on the Roof.* The main character is a milkman named Tevye. Tevye lives a simple life. He follows the Jewish laws, attends synagogue, and observes the sabbath. But his approach to God is not simple or conventional. He argues with God, especially when life does not go as planned despite his faithfulness. When his town is invaded and his daughter marries someone outside of the community, Tevye turns to God and says, "It's true that we are the chosen people. But once in a while can't you choose someone else?" At other moments in the show, Tevye complains about his fate to God. "Sometimes I think," he says, "when things are too quiet up there, you say to yourself: Let's see, what kind of mischief can I play on my friend, Tevye?"[6]

These missives toward God do not suggest Tevye experienced a loss of faith. To the contrary, they exactly express a faith that God remains interested in the fate of the Jewish people. Jewish consciousness of their burden as God's chosen people translated into a willingness to argue with God when they were suffering on God's behalf.

This engaged arguing with God has its roots, I suspect, in part in Jews' experience of suffering. That suffering enabled—perhaps required—Jews to develop a comfort with doubt and struggle. Jews don't expect that God will always offer easy answers, and so Jews have become comfortable with challenging God even as they remained observant of religious laws. And yet, a model of arguing with God far outdates modern Jewish suffering. In the Bible, God's closest friends question God's decisions.

For example, after the Israelites construct a golden calf in place of God while Moses is atop Mount Sinai, God tells Moses of a desire to destroy the Israelites and begin a new people from Moses. Moses tells God that would be a mistake. The other peoples in the world, Moses says to God, know that you have chosen the Jewish people and made them your own. If you destroy them, what will the other nations think about you and your wisdom in choosing the Jews (Exodus 32:9-14)? This remarkable dialogue not only reveals Moses's understanding of divine psychology. It also suggests God is open to human suggestions. Even more so, the survival of God's chosen people depends on God listening to their voices. In this text, God depends on Moses to temper God's own anger.

In their commentaries on the Bible, the Jewish sages come up with a phrase for this approach to God: *chutzpah klappei shamayim*. It means "chutzpah toward heaven." God has chosen the Jews to display *chutzpah* everywhere in life—including toward God.

CONCLUSION

Many Christians at churches where I have spoken have asked me about the idea of the chosen people. What does it mean? I hope I have shown that chosenness has meant many different things to Jews across the centuries. But it's not just the historical perspective on chosenness that matters to Christians and Jews today. All of us—whether Christian or not, Jewish or not, or committed to no religion in particular—can draw guidance from Jewish understandings of chosenness because each of us has had experiences in life of choosing meaning, and each of us has experiences of being chosen by a person or an institution for a particular role or task. Every friendship, for example, involves both choosing and being chosen. A close friendship or a marriage can be sustained through difficult times by the feeling that each person is sacred to—is chosen for—one another. Jews remained committed to God through persecution because we understood ourselves as having a sacred special relationship with God. And each of us can gain in hope and perspective in our religious struggles from the Jewish story. Our relationship with God may not seem perfect and predictable all the time. But by creating us as we are, God chose us. And we choose God by staying in relationship.

God chose Israel for a particular covenantal relationship, but God also chose to create each one of us and to give us each individual characteristics. The Talmud makes this point when it poses the question, "How is God different from a coinmaker?" How did the rabbis answer? "When a coinmaker mints coins," they said, "they all come out the same. When God makes human beings, we all come out differently." God chose each of us to embody the ways we are different from others. In other words, the unique gifts we have are the ones the world needs. God chose each of us to bring them into the world.

For many Jews, our relationship with God plays itself out in the ancient Jewish homeland of Israel. Remember, when God chose Abraham, God also promised a physical homeland. Abraham's descendants would dwell in that land. It is at that subject—the relationship between Jews and the land of Israel—that we next look.

~~~~~~~~

4

ISRAEL

~~~~~~~~

When I was sixteen, my eighty-one-year-old grandpa took two cousins and me to Israel. It was his second visit and our first. The flight was long. Six-foot-three and increasingly frail, my grandpa was uncomfortable. I was worried about how he would feel as we got off the plane, stood for a long time at customs and border check-in, waited for our bags, and boarded a bus for another long ride to our hotel. Yet, as the plane landed, I noticed a big smile on his face. As we walked off the plane, I noticed a spryness, an energy to his step. When we entered the terminal, he stooped down and kissed the ground. Tears filled his eyes. I had never seen him so emotional.

His reaction is not unusual. Many Jews from around the world feel an emotional connection to Israel. Even some who have never been there tear up when they hear Israel's national anthem, "Hatikvah," the hope. What explains this connection to the land? How has it survived over thousands of years, most of which did not see many Jews living in the land itself? How can a religion be so connected to a particular land? And what role does Israel play in Jewish life today?

THE FIRST PROMISE

When God chooses Abraham to begin a new nation, God also makes two promises. God promises Abraham land, and

God promises Abraham descendants. The land promised is called Canaan, and it is a particular slice of land between the Jordan River and the Mediterranean Sea. God instructs Abraham to journey to that land. What will happen when he gets there is not explained. But after Abraham arrives at Canaan, and then leaves soon thereafter because of a famine, we glimpse a theme of Jewish history: Jewish dwelling in the land will not be easy or straightforward. Abraham and his descendants do not simply march into the land, conquer it, and dwell there in peace. Rather, Abraham arrives, leaves, and journeys back. His son Isaac also leaves and returns. And grandson Jacob begins his life there, leaves, returns, and then ultimately dies in Egypt.

It is not until the Israelites experience slavery in Egypt and then journey across the wilderness that they settle as a people in the land of Israel. Their arrival and conquest of the land introduces several critical themes. The first is that Judaism dwells more in community than theology. The laws Moses receives at Mount Sinai are addressed to the Israelites as a people. Many of the laws—including much of the Book of Leviticus—only make sense in the context of a people living in a land. Thus, Jews are a nation with a religion. A nation needs a land to live and carry out the laws God reveals to them. It is only when the Israelites arrive in the land that they can begin to carry out the religious mission God gave them.

The significance of the land itself shapes Jewish practices. For example, Jews can never technically own the land because it belongs to God. Leviticus 25:23 says, "The land must not be permanently sold because the land is mine and you are but strangers and sojourners with Me" (author's translation).

Even today, in modern Israel, only a tiny portion of the land is privately owned. Most of it is owned by the government or nonprofit agencies and is leased to individuals, who then can buy and sell their leases as they would in a free market. My rabbinical seminary, for example, has leased the land on which the school stands for one dollar a year for one hundred years. In other words, the land belongs to God, and we are stewards of it.

This foundational belief leads to other practices like the sabbatical and the Jubilee. The sabbatical was the practice of forgiving debts every seven years. In the Bible, during the Jubilee year—which happened after seven sabbatical years— all the land would be returned to its original tribal owners. Scholars debate whether these practices were consistently followed. But the underlying idea helps us understand the Jewish attachment and view of the land. The land should not become a source of abuse or poverty. It belongs to God, and God apportions it to the entire Jewish people.

The fact that land could not be permanently owned also introduces a degree of equality into Judaism. There was no aristocracy that controlled the land and the wealth. Yes, there was corruption; yes, there were times when wealth became concentrated into a few hands. But the overall thrust of Jewish history was one in which a rough equality and interdependence predominated. The kinds of hierarchies that developed in other societies did not arise in Israel. That remains true today. In the army, for example, there is no custom of saluting those of higher rank. It simply is not part of the culture. This rough equality is also captured in a wonderful quip attributed to Israel's first prime minister, David Ben-Gurion. Ben-Gurion was visiting the United

States, in part to lobby President Eisenhower for economic assistance. At one point during their meeting, Eisenhower said, "It's very difficult to be the president of 170 million people." Ben-Gurion responded, "You think that's hard? It's a lot harder to be the prime minister of two million prime ministers!"[1] We are a people of strong and opinionated individuals who seek to maintain a degree of political and social equality.

It was not only the practices like Jubilee and sabbatical that reinforced a feeling of equality. It was also the nature of the land itself. I first learned and appreciated this truth on a trip to Israel. I was taking a group from my congregation, and we had a tour guide who grew up in Israel and also worked as an archaeologist. It seemed he knew every nook and cranny of the land. He talked extensively about the water supply and the significance that bodies of water like the Sea of Galilee played in ancient Israelite life. Life depended on the annual rainfall. And that was out of the control of the people. The rain did not discriminate between the rich and the poor, the priest or the regular Israelite. The shared dependence encouraged a rough equality because everyone rejoiced when it rained and joined together to gather the rainwater and use it effectively.

Water ultimately became a potent symbol within Jewish life. It served as a metaphor for the Torah. Just as water nourishes and gives us life, so does God's Word. And water came to feature in Jewish ritual practice, in the *mikvah*, a body of natural water in which Jews immerse themselves before holidays and significant life events. In Christianity, baptism—and thus Christian identity and belonging—turns on water. Water became a sacred vessel in religions that developed in the land of Israel in part because water is so precious to the people living there.

CROSSROADS

Another particular attribute of the Promised Land is its position as a global crossroads. On its western border is the Mediterranean Sea, which connects to Europe. East of Israel leads us toward Asia, and the southern border leads toward Africa. Thus, Israel is the only land through which those three continents connect. Also, Israel is only one of two countries where one can avoid going around the southernmost point of Africa and still ship goods to India and China. Those goods would be dropped off in the Mediterranean coast town of Jaffa and moved to the southern tip of Israel and then be shipped to the East Coast of Africa and eventually to India and China. By land and by sea, international merchants traveled through ancient Israel. They carried messages and goods through Israel to the world.

The land's geographic centrality led to intellectual and cultural percolation that in turn shaped the development of Judaism—and that is part of *why* the God of the Bible chose this particular land, and not some other, for the Jewish people. Among the first words God says to Abraham is "Through you all the nations of the world will be blessed" (Genesis 12:3, author's translation). By situating the Jewish people in this central crossroads of humanity, God made that vision more likely. The many biblical references where God says, "My name shall be known among the nations of the world," suggest that the Jewish people's homeland was strategically chosen for that purpose. The many peoples passing through it would help spread God's name to the world.

HISTORY

Even more important than these geographic peculiarities are the events that transpired in Israel; it is those events that so tie the Jewish people to Jerusalem and its sacred sites. To understand this enduring connection, think of your childhood home. It is the family dinners we ate there and the family fights we fought there, the birthdays celebrated, and football games watched and knees skinned and bedtime stories told there, that continue to attach us years after we have moved away to the home where we grew up. A place becomes sacred through events—and not only the happy events—that happen there and the memories we have of them.

Most of the events of the Bible happen in, or on a journey toward, the land of Israel. For example, the temple that Solomon constructed in Jerusalem finds its echo in the Western Wall that remains in the center of Jerusalem. (That particular wall was not part of Solomon's temple but is the only physical reminder of the second temple built after Solomon's was destroyed. Seeing it makes us think of all the stories we read in the Bible that happened in that place.) Walking through the city of David—the center of the Jerusalem during the time of King David—prompts me to think of the story of David and Goliath and of David's dancing with the Ark of the Covenant through the streets of Jerusalem. Crawling through the water tunnel built by

King Hezekiah leads me to recall the miraculous defense of Jerusalem mounted by Hezekiah against the Assyrians in the eighth century BCE. Walking through the heat of Jerusalem during the summer makes me imagine how the fiery words of the biblical prophets echoed in the hearts of the ancient Israelites.

The Bible comes to life in a vivid way in Israel, and these echoes are felt not only by Jews. On an interfaith trip I led, we got off the bus at spot where Jesus delivered the Sermon on the Mount. We thought about the way the topography would have allowed his voice to be carried and heard. We walked by the Sea of Galilee and went into the towns where Jesus preached. We then sat down in a circle and both the church members and synagogue members talked about what they'd felt as they walked through those sites.

The feeling of closeness to Jesus predominated in the words of our Christian participants. I wondered, at first, if our Jewish pilgrims would feel uncomfortable with this intensity of Christian emotion. Would they feel that their homeland was being appropriated by another community? In fact, the Jewish participants said that their Christian friends' responses to the landscape made them feel even more proud of the land of Israel because it was the birthplace of a religion that shaped the lives of billions of people throughout the world.

You may be thinking, *OK, I get the history. But what explains the passionate persistence of the tie to the land in the present day?* Few descendants of Italian or Swedish immigrants to America, after all, feel similar passion about or devote significant resources to supporting and visiting their country of origin. Yet most American Jews—even those who never come to pray at a synagogue—follow the news from Israel closely and feel pride in its accomplishments. This connection is even more surprising because few of them have any ancestors who lived in Israel in recent memory. For most of Jewish history, the vast majority of Jews lived outside of the land of Israel. Yet, our connection to it persisted and continues to do so. Why?

One reason is Israel's centrality to the biblical story of Abraham and Sarah and their descendants, as we have discussed. A second reason is our Jewish liturgy. Jews pray from a fixed liturgy, as we will see in chapter 7. We say the same prayers at the same times throughout the year, with special inserts for different holidays. Many of the prayers recall our connection to the land of Israel. We pray that God will gather up those exiled from Israel and bring us back together in the land. We face east toward Jerusalem during prayer. And in corporate worship we continually read from the Bible whose stories take place in the land of Israel. Prominent twelfth-century writer Judah HaLevi described the feeling of many Jews throughout history when he said, "I am in the West, but my heart is in the East." (The East refers to the land of Israel.)

Israel became a central focus of Jewish prayer after most Jews had migrated from the land in the first and second centuries of the Common Era. Those who left and their descendants still viewed Israel as the holy land, and not simply the source of their ethnicity. They developed the view that when they truly followed God's will and observed the laws of the Torah, God would rebuild the land of Israel and restore the people to it. Until then, Jews were to follow the laws, live as a religious minority, and get along peacefully with others wherever they lived. A return to the land would go hand in hand with the arrival of the messiah.

It always strikes me as remarkable that the Jewish people maintained such a strong ritual connection to land they were physically separated from; it's a remarkable demonstration of the power of faith and history. One reason, I think, that Jews survived through times of persecution was that they could picture in their mind's eye—and daily prayer impressed that image in their hearts—an eventual return to the land of Israel. And that return ultimately happened. There's a profound lesson here for people of all faiths. It's a lesson about what constitutes a miracle. Miracles do not necessarily come out of nowhere. They do not just appear. Faith makes miracles possible. The faith sustained by the Jewish people through prayer and action led to the miracle of the resurgence of the Jewish state in 1948. We do not always know when miracles will arrive. God's timeline is not necessarily our timeline. But we have the power—and perhaps the responsibility—to sustain the faith that makes those miracles possible. Prime Minister David Ben-Gurion captured this when he said: "In Israel, in order to be a realist you must believe in miracles."[2] The miracle of Israel emerged out of the faith of the Jewish people.

A NEW WAY OF THINKING

This theology of longing for the land while building communities outside it persisted until the end of the nineteenth century. It was then that a broad-based movement urging

Jews to return to Israel and build a state there developed around the world. This was the beginning of the Zionist movement, and its origins lay in the growth and increasing virility of anti-Semitism.

Jews, as a group, have always faced hostility and hatred from others. But with the beginning of the Enlightenment in the eighteenth century and the vision of political freedom embodied in the French Revolution, many European Jews felt a new hope that discrimination against them would diminish. Rather than decline, however, it expanded. Instead of seeing Jews as inferior because of their religion, many Europeans began to see Jews as an inferior race and culture. Religious difference was now seen as immutable racial difference. Even the word *anti-Semitism*, which was first used in Germany in 1871, captures the nationalist dimension of this new persecution of Jews: the animus was not directed against a religion, Judaism, but against a racialized way of imagining a people, Semites.

Many Jews throughout Europe gave up on the idea of living peacefully and without persecution in their native countries, and instead began to explore a return to their biblical homeland. Some continued to argue that only God could restore the Jewish homeland. But many turned to a Jewish principle known as *pikuach nefesh*. This is the idea that the saving of life trumps other values. We can set aside certain laws in order to save lives. Jewish life was threatened by the persistence, and vehemence, of anti-Semitism. If returning to the Jewish homeland and building a state there could save lives, God permitted us to pursue it.

This quest took on greater urgency after the Holocaust. Six million Jews had been murdered. The establishment of the Jewish state in 1948 symbolized a national rebirth. Many Jews felt they could only avoid another Holocaust by establishing a strong state governed and defended by Jews themselves. Even many Jews who identified strongly as American or Australian felt a kinship for Israel because they understood, in the shadow of World War II, that Jews had no safe place to live.

Israel's wars and success in defending itself deepened this kinship in the early days of Israel's existence. The grandfather who took me to Israel had also visited there with my grandmother in the late 1950s; he told me that when they were there, they sensed an idealism and a willingness to sacrifice—qualities they didn't perceive in America. Israel was a pioneering country, and the Jews living there knew the future of the world's oldest religion rested on their shoulders.

NEW CHALLENGES

Even as it renewed Judaism, Israel also raised new questions and challenges. How should Jews living in other countries balance commitment to Israel with loyalty to their native country? Must all Jews support the political leadership of the Jewish state? Must Israel accept significant numbers of immigrants from other countries, given how so many Jews were turned away from other countries during the Holocaust? What is the connection between Jews in Israel and Jews in other countries?

These are hard questions without easy answers, and I face them from both members of my congregation and at churches where I speak. Yet all of them pale in the face of the questions surrounding the relationships between Jews in Israel and their Arab neighbors. When early Zionists began to migrate to Palestine in the 1880s, they did not simply take possession of barren land. They created an agency, called the Jewish National Fund, that purchased the land from its owners. Many of the owners lived outside of the land, and much of the land purchased was uninhabited and filled with swamps. Yet, even though land was not stolen, the arrival of significant numbers of European Jews created the conditions of conflict with the Arab people already living in Palestine. These conflicts led to the United Nations proposing a partition of Palestine into two states: one for Jews and the other for Arabs. The Partition of 1947 was accepted by delegates for the proposed Jewish state, but rejected by those of the potential Arab state. Thus, when British control over Palestine officially ended in May 1948, the leaders of the Zionist movement passed a Declaration of Independence and began the processes of government for the officially recognized Jewish state. War with neighboring Arab states followed immediately. The war ended and Israel survived, but lost 1 percent of its population (6,373 soldiers and civilians); about 7,000 Arabs were killed.

The state grew and gathered Jewish immigrants from around the world. In 1967, another war threatened the country, but Israel emerged from this war with a wide-ranging victory. When the war ended after six days of fighting on June 10, 1967—its short duration earned it the name the Six-Day War—Israel controlled three times the amount of territory than the original size of the country. This rapid and unexpected victory changed not only the size of the country.

It also changed the way many Jews saw themselves and the future of Judaism.

Some Jews, for example, saw Israel's overwhelming victory as a sign from God that the promised messiah was preparing to arrive. In order to hasten his arrival, it was incumbent upon Jews to settle the entire biblical land of Israel, much of which had been captured during the war. This is the origin of what today are called the Settlements.

Israel's victories also united the many Jews who had seen the prospect of Israel's loss in the Six-Day War as a potential second Holocaust. Many American Jews who had previously felt only marginally connected to Israel found their connection to the nation quickened once the country was threatened by its neighbors. They compared Israel to the biblical David and the surrounding Arab states as the biblical Goliath. Older members of my own synagogue tell the story about a man in the community who was Jewish but had never been involved in Jewish activities. He was very wealthy and came from a family that had rejected religion and even changed their last name so they wouldn't be identified as Jewish. On the second day of the Six-Day War, this man came into the synagogue. He handed the rabbi a check for $100,000 and said, "Please get it to the right people in Israel." On the next sabbath, he attended the synagogue for the first time in his life.

PILGRIMAGES TO THE HOMELAND

After the Six-Day War, many synagogues made a visit to Israel part of their educational curriculum. At my synagogue, for example, for several decades any teen who completed the high school educational program would receive a free trip to Israel from the congregation. The rabbinical seminary I attended also required a year of study in Israel. In 2000, a group of Jewish philanthropists created a program called Birthright Israel, whereby every Jewish person under age twenty-six could visit Israel for ten days at no cost. The name of the program illustrates its religious significance: It suggests that every Jewish person has an inherent connection to the land of Israel. It is part of their birthright. These trips function in a way similar to a pilgrimage in Christianity or Islam. When we visit Israel, we ascend to a sacred place. Since its inception, Birthright has brought over 650,000 Jews to Israel.[3]

In 2018, some participants on Birthright trips began a protest that illustrates one of the core challenges facing Jews today. Several groups of participants walked off the tour to protest Israel's continual control of territory populated primarily by Arabs known as Palestinians. Israel's continual control of and presence in these territories is known as the Occupation, and it has sparked fierce divisions among Jews around the world. Those who oppose the Occupation see it as militaristic and a perversion of the Jewish value of welcoming the stranger and seeing every human being as created in the image of God. Some even compare the Israeli army to the Nazis and the Palestinians to the Jews who were persecuted and murdered by them. Other Jews think settlements provide a necessary defense against terror attacks. They also fulfill the spiritual goal of bringing a Jewish presence to the entire biblical land of Israel.

These are, in some sense, relatively new questions for Judaism. When Jews were a minority who lived under other nations' sovereignty, they did not have to address questions about the use of political and military power. Now we do. My feeling is that Israel has to defend itself, and that, before taking significant risks in the interest of peace, Israeli political leaders need somehow to be sure that their Palestinian and Arab counterparts truly want peace.

To be sure, these are enormously complex questions. I try to let my thinking about them be guided by two teachings that are two thousand years old and that demonstrate the necessity and difficulty of peace and self-defense. The first is found in the Talmud: "If your enemy plans to kill you, arise early and kill him first."[4] This stark teaching—one we might not expect to find in a sacred book—reflects both the Jewish people's constant need for self-defense throughout history and the worldly thrust of Jewish tradition. The Jewish sages taught the Torah was not written for the heavens. It was written for people on earth. In order to observe the Torah, Jews had to survive as a people. Thus, the imperative to defend oneself, even preemptively, is justified.

The second teaching I hold dear instructs us to "seek peace and pursue it" (Psalm 34:14). The use of two verbs—*seek* and *pursue*—led the Jewish sages to emphasize that one must not only work for peace when others approach us. We must also actively pursue it, looking for creative ways to bring forth peace out of conflict. Thus, in 1978, Israel signed a peace agreement with Egypt, a nation with whom it had fought three wars. In exchange for peace, Israel relinquished control of the Sinai desert, a piece of land bigger than the state of Israel itself. Israelis have tried to combine effective self-defense with the commitment to taking risks for peace.

Still, tension over the Occupation has widened the distance between Israelis and other Jews. Israeli Jews feel most American Jews don't understand the existential threat Israelis face in part because they do not face the same security risks. This tension raises difficult questions: What is the future relationship between American Jews and Israel? How attached do Jews feel to Israel today? And why does it matter?

FAMILY

When I interviewed for my first rabbinic position, the search committee asked how I viewed the state of Israel. I responded, "As family. Israelis are my extended family. Families fight. Families disagree. But families always come around and support one another." That answer reflected the views of most American Jews in the twentieth century. After the Holocaust, American Jews had to do all they could to support our fledging family in Israel. They needed us. And we also needed them. The pioneer spirit of Israel—the David standing up against the Goliath of the Arab Middle East— gave American Jews purpose and hope. Israel renewed Jewish life around the world after the Holocaust.

That feeling lingers today. About one-third of American Jews visit sometime in their life. And 78 percent say a strong Israel is important to the future of Judaism.[5] I see this feeling of attachment at my synagogue—people will always come to a program or class talking about the situation in Israel.

Yet, younger Jews feel less attached to Israel. In part, this is because the more involved one is in the Jewish community, the more one tends to support Israel, and younger Jews are less observant of Jewish religious tradition. But politics also drives younger Jews to a feeling of alienation from Israel. American Jews tend to be politically liberal, while the last several governments in Israel have been politically conservative. Indeed, Israelis have become much more politically conservative over the last fifteen years, in part of because of the multiple failed attempts at peace agreements with the Palestinians. The current prime minister—Benjamin Netanyahu, now Israel's longest-serving prime minister— has not held peace talks for several years; in so doing (or, more to the point, in so *not* doing), Netanyahu has pursued a confrontational policy toward the Palestinians. Some American Jews believe that, in the continued Occupation (that is, the Israeli military presence in and legal authority over parts of the West Bank and Jerusalem), Israel is moving away from democracy and toward apartheid. Furthermore, many American Jews, including younger American Jews, feel alienated from Israel because Netanyahu is closely aligned with the Republican Party in America. (One sociologist described American Jews a "blue state" and Israel as a "red state.")

But political differences provide only a surface explanation for the deteriorating relationship between younger American Jews and Israel. Perhaps the most obvious explanation for younger American Jews' diminished commitments to Israel is that Judaism has different meanings for Americans and for Israelis. For most American Jews—not for the Orthodox, who constitute about 10 percent of American Jewish population, but for most everyone else—Judaism is an important, but decidedly secondary, component of their identity. People attend synagogue occasionally. They feel proud of being Jewish. But they have many other pursuits in life, and Judaism is just one of many activities. Judaism is a religion they draw upon in times of need; it is not an all-encompassing way of life.

Israeli Judaism is much different. For Israelis, Judaism is everywhere. Judaism shapes their calendar. Most stores are closed on Saturday because of the sabbath. An Israeli Jew may not himself wear a skullcap, but he daily encounters people who do. The TaNaK is part of the public school curriculum. The daily language is the language of the Bible. Even Israelis who rarely visit a synagogue are surrounded by the symbols and practices of traditional Judaism.

When Israel was threatened and needed the support of American Jews, the relationship between Israeli Jews and American Jews strengthened. "We are one" was a common saying for American and Israeli Jews after the Six-Day War in 1967. Today, however, an economically and militarily strong Israel has a less dire need for American Jews' support. Sadly, at least to me, Israeli and American Jews increasingly march to different drumbeats. I fear that in the coming decades the American Jewish community will, on the whole, grow more distant from Israel.

While this growing divide saddens me, I also see it in the context of Jewish history. For 3,500 of our 4,000 years, Jews have been spread out across many geographic areas. That geographical diversity allowed the Jewish people to survive because the persecution of one community did not destroy the entire religion. In addition, Jewish cultural expression benefited from the unique customs of different geographic communities.

The interaction between various Jewish communities also made Jews a global people long before the era of globalization began in the twentieth century. Thus, a modern Judaism with multiple geographic centers—the United States and Israel, Tel Aviv and New York—is consistent with the pattern and best practices of Jewish history. Israel is the Holy Land, and Jewish life there will always be of central importance to worldwide Judaism. But a Judaism that thrives in multiple places means Jews can continue to develop unique cultural practices and contribute to American (and British and French and Australian and Canadian) life.

Even as the relationship between American Jews and Israel has weakened, the relationship between Israeli and American Christians has strengthened over the last several decades. During my last trip to Israel, the tour guide told me that over the last few years, he had taken tens of thousands of Christians on tours of Israel. And he was only one guide. His experience reflects the growth of Christian Zionism in the United States. These are Christians—mostly, but not exclusively, self-identified evangelicals—who visit Israel, support Israeli charities, and even celebrate some traditionally Jewish holidays like Passover. One of the biblical verses cited in justification for these practices is Genesis 12:3 when God says to Abraham, "I will bless those who bless you and curse those you curse you" (BSB).

Visiting Israel, purchasing products from Israel and supporting Israel's political and social needs serve as ways for Christians to bless Israel. Having spoken at dozens of churches, I know how genuine this support is. While some Jews fear this warmth toward Israel flows from a desire for Jews to convert to Christianity in order to hasten the return of Jesus, I have never experienced this pressure. (And when I've discussed this issue with pastors, my interlocutors usually tell me that they believe that nothing a Christian can do will hasten the return of Jesus; only God can decide when that will happen.) I suspect the relationship between Christians and Israel will continue to deepen because Israel provides a shared geographical focal point. It is the land of the Jews, and it is the land where Jesus lived and taught. While Israel may now divide American Jews, it has served as a bridge between Jews and Christians.

One set of practices uniting Jews in and outside of Israel is celebrating holidays. Israel may be a holy space, but Judaism also resides in holy time. The seventh day of the week is holy, set apart by God for rest, study, and worship. And several days throughout the year are sacred. It is to Jewish holy days and their customs that we now turn.

5

The Calendar

Autumn Holidays

One of the most striking features of Judaism is our calendar. Our traditional calendar is different from the
calendar the secular Western world lives by: ours is based
on the lunar cycle rather than the Gregorian model. Thus,
there are 355 days in a year rather than 365. That means the
holidays every year fall on different dates on the Gregorian
calendar. In order to ensure the Jewish and Gregorian calen-
dars do not fall too far out of alignment, we add seven extra
months to the calendar every nineteen years. Thus, the winter holiday of Chanukah may fall some years in November,
but it will usually fall in December but never in July. In this
chapter you'll learn how this calendar works and what morsels of ancient Jewish wisdom it might yield.

Also notable is the structure of a Jewish day. The Jewish
day begins at night. When the sun falls, the date changes.
That way of counting stems from the Bible. In the creation
story, we read, "And it was evening, and it was morning, a
first day" (author's translation). The evening comes before
the morning. Thus, the day begins in the evening. The
evening officially begins when we can see three stars in the
sky. Consequently, the Jewish sabbath begins in the evening,
at sundown on Friday, and ends at sundown on Saturday.
All other Jewish holidays follow this same pattern.

A nineteenth-century rabbi said, "For the Jew, the
calendar is his catechism."[1] That is, how we use our time
reveals and shapes our values, our commitments, and our

beliefs. Think about your own life. Do you devote most of your time to work? To family? Do you pass the weekend watching sports or going to the theater or running errands? Time is the most precious resource in the world because we can never make more of it. We can make more money. We can find new sources of income. But we can never make more time.

The Jewish sages organized the Jewish calendar to emphasize particular events and values throughout the year. Thus, understanding the Jewish way of organizing time reveals core beliefs and values. Central among them is an embrace of freedom. One of the definitions of freedom is control over one's time. A slave's time is controlled by others. A free person decides how to fill her own time.

According to the Jewish sages, after freeing the Israelites from Egypt, the first commandment God gave the people was the commandment to establish a calendar. The priority of this commandment underscores the way time distinguishes the enslaved from the free: God wanted the Israelites to *immediately* unlearn the posture of following a calendar that someone else set and to begin to craft a way of inhabiting time that oriented them toward God and toward neighbor in a life-giving blend of work and rest.

The calendar ancient Israel established was divided into twelve months of twenty-nine or thirty days. The arrival of the new moon began a new month. Scholars disagree about why exactly the moon was central in Israel's timekeeping. Some suggest that the ancestors of the Israelites worshipped the moon as the representation of God in the world. Indeed, many groups in the ancient Near East venerated the moon, and the name of Abraham's father and his uncle suggest they may have come from a moon-worshipping background in the town of Haran. Abraham's father was named Terach, which is virtually identical to one of the Hebrew words meaning moon. Abraham's uncle is named Laban, which is another word for moon.

Why does this all matter for understanding Judaism? Well, the moon has long been seen as the lesser star. It is less prominent than the sun. The Jewish people have always been a small people, rarely the majority where they live. And the Bible frequently elevates the younger child over the older. Think of Isaac over Ishmael, Jacob over Esau, Joseph over his brothers, even Moses over Aaron. Judaism reverses the usual order of things. Worshipping the moon over the brighter sun fits within this pattern, so the basic structure of the calendar embodies a core component of Israel's identity.

ROSH HASHANAH

In the calendar of the secular West, January 1 is the first day of the new year. The first day of the Jewish New Year (which usually falls in September) is called Rosh Hashanah, literally "Head of the Year."

On Rosh Hashanah the primary theme is renewal. The new year is counted from the date of the creation of the world. As I finish this book, we just entered into the year 5880. That means that, according to the biblical chronology, God created the world 5880 years ago. One of the central prayers said on Rosh Hashanah proclaims, "Today is the day of creation." Notice it says "today," because creation is both in the past and the present. Creation is continually re-creating, just as the seasons pass and return again in a different form. But we human beings often become blind to God's continual creativity. Therefore, we need a day like Rosh Hashanah to wake us up to it. On Rosh Hashanah, instead of drinking champagne and partying and becoming numb to the world, we listen to the sound of the shofar—a ram's horn used on Rosh Hashana as a trumpet, which is like a ritual alarm clock. That harsh sound is meant to cut through all the busyness of everyday life. The shofar, which is blown one hundred times throughout Rosh Hashana, wakes us up from the spiritual slumber of taking God's creation for granted. We are meant to remember what a blessing it is to be alive and the responsibility we have to express gratitude to God for the gift of life.

The shofar also serves as a proclamation of God's sovereignty. At royal coronation ceremonies, we still hear the sound of trumpets. Rosh Hashanah is an annual coronation ceremony for God, as the Jewish people proclaim God as their monarch. One of the central prayers of Rosh Hashanah is called *Avinu Malkanu*, which means "Our father, our king." The entire congregation reads the prayer pleading with "Our father, our king" to forgive us for our sins and bless us with prosperity and joy in the year ahead. Every year, when my congregation recites this prayer, people break down in tears. Americans, of course, don't know much about having a king, but something in the prayer's assertion of a loving sovereign who hears the pleas of the people is stirring and speaks to our deep need to know that we are loved and cared for.

Rosh Hashanah is also known by the Jewish sages as Yom HaZikaron, which means "Day of Memory." The specific memory echoed on Rosh Hashanah is Abraham's faithfulness to God atop Mount Moriah. God asked Abraham to bind his son Isaac and offer him as a sacrifice. When Abraham followed God's instructions and prepared to sacrifice his son, God stopped him, teaching us that God does not desire human sacrifice, which a common practice in the ancient Near East. Abraham sacrifices a ram in Isaac's place. The shofar—the ram's horn—reminds us of his faithfulness.

This theme of memory remains one of the most powerful for Jews on Rosh Hashanah. We come to the synagogue to remember ancestors. We also come to remember key moments in our history. Rosh Hashanah is a two-day holiday, and in 2018, the second day of Rosh Hashanah was Tuesday, September 11. Memory resonated in multiple ways that day. A friend who is also a rabbi decided to explore the meaning of memory on Rosh Hashanah outside of the synagogue. He led his congregation in prayer on the first day of Rosh Hashanah. But on the second day, he went to various well-known sites in New York. He wore traditional Jewish garb. And he said a Jewish prayer known as the Mourner's Kaddish. Jews say the Mourner's Kaddish every year on the anniversary of the death of a loved one. He wrote about his experience, and when he said the Mourner's Kaddish at the New York stock exchange shortly before the day's trading began, he said that, "With the exception of some machines that kept chirping, not a person made a sound. . . . Even with its flashing screens and inglorious reputation, the stock exchange had—if only for a moment—something holy in its midst."[2] Memory touches each of us. What we remember shapes who we are. Rosh Hashanah reminds us to remember the role of God in our lives and the life of our community.

YOM KIPPUR

Eight days after Rosh Hashanah is Yom Kippur, the Day of Atonement. The days in between—along with Rosh Hashanah and Yom Kippur themselves—are called the Days of Awe. Most Jews consider Yom Kippur the most important holiday of the year. We fast the entire day. We also spent most of it in the synagogue, either in prayer or study. Yom Kippur is the one day when even those Jews who feel very little connection to their religion come to the synagogue and pray. This fits with one of themes of Yom Kippur: return and forgiveness. God accepts as we are, and Yom Kippur is an opportunity to return to God and to the right path.

Although it may be odd for a rabbi to think about Jesus on the holiest day of the Jewish year, I often find myself thinking on Yom Kippur of one of Jesus's parables: the story of the prodigal son. The younger son has left home and lived a life of sin. When he cannot go on anymore, he returns home, and his father welcomes him. That's what God does for us on Yom Kippur. God welcomes us—whomever we are and wherever we have been.

One of the core prayers expressing this idea is called *Kol Nidre*, meaning "All our vows." The prayer asks God to annul our vows during the coming year if, despite our best efforts, we are unable to keep them. Scholars speculate the prayer began during the Spanish inquisition, when Jews who were forced to convert to Christianity in public continued to maintain their Judaism in private. *Kol Nidre* was the prayer they said asking God for forgiveness for the sins they would have to commit during the coming year. Because of its importance, the *Kol Nidre* is said three times. In Judaism, three times is a signal of intent. Saying the *Kol Nidre* three times signals our true intention to welcome everyone into the community and seek absolution when we do not fulfill our vows.

In some synagogues in the nineteenth and twentieth centuries, the *Kol Nidre* was eliminated from the worship service, because some members of the Jewish community feared that it might be used to promote an anti-Semitic charge that Jews did not have to keep their promises. The prayer, of course, never had that intent. *Kol Nidre* is about the reality that sometimes we cannot fulfill our obligations no matter how hard we try. People were so attracted to the *Kol Nidre* praycr that they protested when some rabbis took it out of the service, and it was restored. Today many synagogues also listen to a musical version of the prayer written by Max Bruch and played on the cello. It begins in a minor key and ends in a major one, reflecting the evolution of our emotions on Yom Kippur. We begin with pain and hope for forgiveness and end with joy as God forgives and welcomes each of us.

The *Kol Nidre* service happens in the evening, when the Jewish day begins. The next morning we gather again in prayer. The core prayers are confessional in nature. We note the different types of sins we have committed. I use the word *sin* because it is the closest English equivalent to the Hebrew word *chet*. But every translation is, in some way, a distortion because Hebrew words usually have multiple meanings. The word *chet* means "missing the mark." When we are confessing sins, we are acknowledging times we missed the mark in our relationships, in our responsibilities to other human beings and God. That means something different than sin because the word *sin* rests on the idea of human sinfulness. That is, in many Christian theologies, we commit sins because it is part of human beings' sinful nature to do so. But in Judaism a chet is not an expression of an inherent sinfulness. We will miss the mark not because we are fallen but because perfection is an unattainable ideal. Yet we repent of our *chetayim* (plural for chet) because we recognize that, even if perfection is not attainable, we can change our behavior; we can grow through prayer, study and action.

Like Rosh Hashanah, Yom Kippur includes a reading from the Torah, Deuteronomy 29:9–30:20. Here, God speaks through Moses to the entire Jewish people. This reading for Yom Kippur is the only one where Moses specifically addresses men, women, and children—it even mentions the "one who draws your water" and "the one who chops your wood" (Deuteronomy 29:11 ESV). That is the biblical way of saying every person needs to hear these words—rich and poor, friends and enemies, young and old. Even future generations who are not alive to physically hear those words from Moses are still symbolically present. The dimension of time does not apply to God's Word, as the Bible says, "This is addressed to those who are not here with us" (Deuteronomy 29:15, author's translation).

This moment is an important one. Moses is about to communicate God's Word. So what does God say? God tells the Jewish people to "choose life" (Deuteronomy 30:19).

That seems like a rather vague commandment. But Moses goes further to explain that choosing life means following the mitzvot, the commandments God has revealed to the Jewish people. It is to trust that those commandments are the path to a meaningful life. The people are preparing to enter into the Promised Land, and the generation before them had perished because they did not trust God's promise to lead them across the wilderness. In effect, they chose death when they built and worshipped the golden calf. This new generation has the chance to make a better choice. They can heed Moses and "choose life" by following God's commandments.

This section from Deuteronomy is not the only biblical reading for Yom Kippur. It is paired with a text from the Book of Isaiah (Isaiah 57:14–58:14). That text (which some Christians read on Ash Wednesday) lambasts meaningless fasting. Consider the context for a moment. On a day when everyone is fasting, we read a biblical text saying God does not want fasting if it is not accompanied by life-affirming action. Feeding the hungry, clothing the naked, freeing the oppressed—these are the deeds of real atonement. One nineteenth-century rabbi said most people worry about their own bodies and other people's souls. Yom Kippur reminds us to worry about our own souls and other people's bodies.

One of the ways we examine our souls is to look back on our actions over the year. The Hebrew name for this process is a *cheshbon hanefesh*. The word *cheshbon* means "bill" or "accounting statement." *Nefesh* means "soul." An accountant draws up a complete inventory of expenses and expenditures, looking at where to save money or spend less. On Yom Kippur, we do the same thing with our actions. We take a complete inventory and try to see where we can live more ethically and draw closer to God. We do an accounting of our soul. It is not always an easy process. The longer I have been a rabbi, the more I have seen how powerful willful ignorance and denial are. It is easier to pretend we did not do something than it is to grapple with why we did it and how we can change. For example, I like to think of myself as someone who never loses his cool. I am generally calm and easygoing and am proud of being that way. If someone mentions a time I lost my temper, my initial impulse is to deny it. It doesn't fit the way I think about myself. This is why I need the discipline of *cheshbon hanefesh*. I need to do a thorough accounting so I don't miss anything. I need this time of year for self-examination so I don't conveniently ignore what makes me uncomfortable. Yom Kippur is a gift in that it provides a time and space for me to do so.

After conducting a *cheshbon hanefesh*, what do we do with what we discover? Once again the Jewish sages provide direction by distinguishing between two types of sins. The first are sins against another human being. That could mean lying or stealing or injuring with words or deeds. The second are sins against God: not saying the required prayers or fulfilling our obligations for worship or ritual behavior. For the first type of sin, we need to ask the injured person for forgiveness. God cannot forgive us until we have sought forgiveness from the person we hurt. For the second type of sin, God forgives the moment we ask.

When I have talked about these two types of sins at churches, some people ask why God can't forgive us for all sins. Isn't God all-powerful and full of grace and kindness? And what happens if the injured person refuses to forgive us? Are we stuck in a state of permanent guilt? According to the rabbinic sages, we have an obligation to seek forgiveness from someone we have hurt. If they refuse, we seek it again. If they refuse again, we seek it a third time. If they refuse then—and if we have expressed and felt remorse and done all we can to repair the relationship and make financial amends if appropriate—then we are forgiven. God serves as a proxy in place of the injured person and forgives us on their behalf. In effect, the Jewish sages are establishing limits for human guilt. We need not live in a state of permanent sinfulness. If we truly seek forgiveness, we will receive it. That is the underlying message of the Day of Atonement.

SUKKOT

Yom Kippur usually ends with a festive gathering where the day's fast is broken and we celebrate a clean slate and fresh start. We also begin immediately constructing a temporary dwelling known as a *sukkah*, which we will inhabit during the very next holiday, Sukkot. Some Jews walk directly from the synagogue to their backyard or balcony and start lifting wood beams and hammering right away. This juxtaposition of the afternoon's Yom Kippur prayers and the evening's hammering highlights the distinction between the spiritual work of the Day of Atonement and the physical work of Sukkot. Both reflect the will of God.

A sukkah is a structure with three walls sturdy enough to withstand normal winds. The roof is made of organic material with enough opening to see the sky. Usually we use material like palm leaves, bamboo sticks, and other natural material for the roof. Some Jews will eat, sleep, and spend most of their time for the eight days of Sukkot in the sukkah.

The purpose of living in the sukkah is to remind ourselves of the journey of the Israelites across the wilderness from Egypt to the Promised Land. The Israelites lacked permanent homes. They lived in temporary huts dependent on God's mercy and protection. We remind ourselves of their faith when we do the same.

Sukkot also has a broader message: every person lives in a state of insecurity and uncertainty. We do not know the future. We are exposed to the elements—of the natural world, of other people, of our physical bodies. We may know people who have seemed healthy one day and passed away soon thereafter. Life is uncertain. Nevertheless we rejoice. We pray. We eat. We live. Sukkot is the only holiday in described in the Bible as *zeman simchatenu*, a time of joy (Deuteronomy 16:14). Insecurity does not demand fear. It invites happiness amid a trust in God and God's Word. Faith, as Rabbi Jonathan Sacks has put it, is not certainty. It is the courage to live with uncertainty. That's what Sukkot represents and teaches.[3]

One of the ways we make Sukkot joyful is by inviting people into our sukkah for a meal. In Hebrew the phrase for hospitality is *hachnasat orchim*, and it is one of the practices described in the Jewish happiness prayer. Community is one of the gifts God gives us, and by inviting people into our sukkah, we create bonds that help us navigate the insecurity of life.

The Jewish sages decreed that we read the book of Ecclesiastes during Sukkot in our sukkahs. During my first year in seminary, which I spent in Jerusalem, I would run through the city streets most mornings. Every day during Sukkot I would see dozens of homes with sukkahs out front. In almost every one, I saw at least one person holding a Bible and reading (presumably) from the Book of Ecclesiastes.

Ecclesiastes seems an odd choice for Sukkot. The book is more depressing than uplifting. Ecclesiastes—which is a pen name for King Solomon—suggests life is a meaningless pursuit of vanity and riches. It suggests our actions have no impact on the world, and that "there is nothing new under the sun" (Ecclesiastes 1:9). I remember reading the book fully for the first time in seminary and wondering how to make sense of it because it felt out of sync with the rest of the Bible. The Bible is all about choosing our actions wisely and responding to God's will. Ecclesiastes says it doesn't really matter what we do because everything is meaningless. Why would we read such a book on Sukkot, a time of happiness, and a time we remember God's intervention in history in leading the Israelites across the wilderness from Egypt to the Promised Land?

One answer is that Ecclesiastes suggests life is meaningless when we live it only for ourselves. The word *I* dominates the first half of the book of Ecclesiastes. *I* made, *I* bought, *I* built. Everything centers around King Solomon and what he did for himself. But focusing on ourselves makes us miserable because human beings are social animals. Part of our satisfaction comes from connection to others, and when we focus solely on ourselves, we go against our own nature. The Bible is conveying this truth by connecting King Solomon's misery with his excessive self-interest.

Then the book tells us how to overcome self-interest. Ecclesiastes ultimately overcomes his misery by turning outward and focusing on the present. We already saw one verse where Ecclesiastes notes the power of relationships. Another seminal verse found in the Psalms is, "This is the day that the LORD has made; let us rejoice and be glad in it" (Psalm 118:24 ESV). In Hebrew the word for "the day" is *hayom*, which also means "today." In other words, today is a gift. We do not know about what comes next. Therefore, find joy in it. The way we find joy is in relationships.

We see this truth in the Hebrew word for rejoice, which is *simcha*. It also means "joy" or "happiness." The word *simcha* is typically used to refer to communal gatherings. A simcha is a celebration with others. The presence of others is what makes an event joyful, *sameach*. The word *simcha* appears more times in Ecclesiastes than in any other book of Bible. In Ecclesiastes, Solomon finds happiness by living in the present with other people. That's also what happens on Sukkot. We spend eight days, outside, living in the moment, inviting others in to eat and talk and be with us. It's clear, sitting in a sukkah, in a way that it is not clear inside a snug house, that we cannot control what will happen—we cannot control the wind, the rains; we cannot keep out the critters we usually exclude from our homes. What we can do, however, is invite others to experience the unpredictability with us, and find meaning in eating together, praying together, singing together. We make joy out of life's uncertainties.

SIMCHAT TORAH

Sukkot ends with another time of simcha—a holiday called Simchat Torah, which means "the joy of Torah." On

Simchat Torah we celebrate the completion of the annual reading of the Five Books of Moses. The Jewish sages offer a mystical interpretation of the holiday, suggesting that God was sad to see the end of the rejoicing on Sukkot. Therefore, God added one last holiday of pure joy. Simchat Torah is like an afterparty to a big wedding celebration.

On Simchat Torah Jews gather in the synagogue and read the final verses of the book of Deuteronomy, and then immediately begin reading gate-opening verses of the Book of Genesis. Typically, two Torah scrolls are opened, with one at the end and the other at the beginning. The Torah reader tries to read the last verse of Deuteronomy and first verse of Genesis in one breath. This practice illustrates Jews' ongoing engagement with and love of the Torah. We study it endlessly because its lessons are always relevant and enduring. We will always discover more wisdom in it, and our obligation to read and study it never ends.

In my congregation, on Simchat Torah, I try to cultivate a love of and closeness to Torah. We move all the chairs into the middle of the sanctuary and create a big circle of people. Then I take the Torah scroll, place it in one person's hands, and then unroll the rest of it around the sanctuary. I explain that a scroll is created by sewing together pieces of parchment. I demonstrate the way a full-time professional scribe writes every letter of the Torah by hand—if he makes a mistake, he has to start over the piece of parchment on which he is writing. I tell the community that a special pen is used and a blessing is said every time the name of God is written. I mention that no metal objects are used in the construction and writing of a Torah scroll because metal is used to create weapons and the Torah symbolizes peace.

Then I point out some of the most well-known verses in Torah, like the Ten Commandments and the crossing of the Red Sea. The participants are seeing these stories as they are holding the Torah scroll. It deepens our relationship with God's Word.

Simchat Torah is a fitting cap to the autumn holidays because it brings us back to celebrating the center of Jewish life—the Torah. For millennia Jews have described the Torah as a Tree of Life. For Jews, the Torah is God made incarnate in words. Through those words we glean our beliefs, our practices, our history, our values. Our lives are spent climbing that tree, bringing us closer to God and firmly rooting us in the soil of our ancestors.

Torah also has a critical message today. We live in an era of rapid change. Popular websites like ancestry.com remind us that we know ourselves better—we find greater stability in a fast-moving world—when we have a firmer grasp of our roots. Christianity is rooted in Judaism, and Judaism is rooted in the Torah. To discover our roots is to better understand ourselves and why God put us here.

Torah is not for Jews only. The early Jewish sages said God wrote the Torah in seventy languages. The Torah speaks to us in the language of our own faith and traditions. The more languages in which we can speak it, the more we can fulfill it.

After Simchat Torah, we have a little break—a few months of ordinary time—until the next several holidays. To them we now turn.

6

THE CALENDAR

Winter and Spring Holidays

I recently spent a day visiting with teachers at a local Jewish day school. Such schools teach religious and secular subjects, and the teachers for the secular subjects do not need to be Jewish. As I spoke with one of them, she told me she loves teaching at a Jewish school. I asked why. She echoed much of what I'd heard from other teachers before: the values in the school (there are no locks on the lockers), the academic environment, the sense of service among the students. And then she smiled and said, "And the holidays. We Christians have two big holidays. And one of them is always on a Sunday. You have at least a dozen, and we get all of them off of school!"

It is true. The Jewish calendar has many holidays. And we do not control when they fall. Sometimes they fall during the week and sometimes on weekends. While this may be inconvenient, it also reminds us that we are not in control of everything in the world. Sometimes we need to follow rhythms and scripts we did not create or write. Sometimes our faith requires us to sacrifice convenience or ease.

In 1961, famed Jewish baseball pitcher Sandy Koufax refused to pitch a game during the World Series because it fell on Yom Kippur. As we discussed in the last chapter, Yom Kippur is the holiest day of the year for Jews. Koufax's decision conveyed to the world that certain values matter most. Pitching a game was not worth sacrificing his faith and tradition.

Not all the holidays require us to refrain from work and other activities. But each of them asks us to take time to remember a part of Jewish history and God's role in our lives. This chapter introduces the winter and spring holidays. They all revolve around the concept of freedom. Chanukah celebrates the religious freedom sought by a group of Jews known as the Maccabees. Passover tells the story of the Exodus from Egypt, which has inspired those seeking freedom, from the founding fathers of America to modern civil rights leaders. Shavuot—which means "weeks" and celebrates the moment the Israelites received the Torah at Mount Sinai—highlights the connection between freedom and responsibility. Observing the laws of Torah is the way we sustain the freedom given by God. By the end of this chapter, you will also see the way the Exodus story runs like a thread through the Jewish holidays. It is the foundational story of freedom, and it echoes in our lives today. Ultimately, learning about and experiencing the Jewish holidays will give you a new perspective of what it means to live in relationship to God. The holidays systematically bring us into a dynamic relationship with God and with history. We follow ancient rituals, adding our own creativity and customs to them, and thereby reliving the journey from slavery to freedom.

CHANUKAH

In America, the eight-day holiday Chanukah is well known—but the story behind it less so. Fundamentally, the holiday celebrates the victory of the Jews over a hostile foreign power that was trying to destroy the Jewish people.

Around 160 BCE, a descendant of Alexander the Great named Antiochus controlled Palestine. He began to require Jews to worship Greek gods. He installed a statue of Zeus in the Jerusalem temple. He also forced Jews to compete nude in Olympic games, a practice violating norms of modesty. He pushed for all Jews under his control to dress in Greek styles and make other changes in their culture. It was a form of religious persecution and cultural genocide. Antiochus was trying to destroy the Jewish community and assimilate it into the Greek-speaking peoples, as he had done to other native peoples.

For a while, this strategy worked. Some Jews began to worship in the Hellenistic style. Antiochus was even able to have a high priest appointed who encouraged assimilation into Greek culture. But other Jews began to see Antiochus's efforts for what they were: a way of undermining Judaism and the God of Israel. Tension mounted within the Jewish community. Many Jews in the city embraced Hellenism, but those in the hills of Judea did not. It was in the hilly countryside that the revolt began. A large family of Jews known as the Hasmoneans first challenged other Jewish leaders who had started Hellenistic practices. When their concerns were rejected, they took on the name Maccabee, which is the acronym for the first letters of the words in the Hebrew phrase, "Who is like You among the gods, Adonai, God of Israel?"

After three years of battle, the Maccabees defeated the Jewish Hellenists along with Antiochus and his supporters. They declared independence and established a new Jewish kingdom and high priest. One of their first acts after victory was entering into the temple in Jerusalem and rededicating it to the God of Israel. The rededication involved eight days of singing and feasting. This story is told in the Books of Maccabees, which are not part of the Hebrew Bible but are part of the Catholic and Christian Orthodox Old Testaments. The rededication lasted for eight days because the Maccabees had not been able to celebrate the eight-day biblical holiday of Sukkot while they were in battle. Thus, Chanukah served as a substitute that year for Sukkot, and soon become a regular holiday celebrating the victory.

During the time of the Maccabees and the first few centuries thereafter, Chanukah was primarily a military celebration. It honored the fighting prowess and spirit of the Maccabees. After a couple of other Israelite revolts against Rome failed—first between 66 and 70 CE and again in 130 CE—the Jewish sages decided to tone down the military focus of the holiday and emphasize instead its spiritual message. They wrote down and taught a story not recorded in the Books of Maccabees; it may have been folk legend.

The story is that the Maccabees entered the temple after conquering it from Antiochus. Their leader, Judah, ordered that the temple be cleansed of all Hellenistic influences and ritual items. He restored the menorah to its rightful place. But the Maccabees had to find oil to light the menorah, and all they could find was a tiny jar. The oil in the jar, however, burned for eight days. It was a miracle, and it set the precedent for the rededication holiday lasting for eight days, with candles lit every evening.

The candles are lit from left to right, and an additional candle is added for each night. The candles are lit by a head candle, known in Hebrew as a *shamash*, which is kindled every night. Each additional candle represents another of the eight days, and together they symbolize a brighter future. Sometimes we are tempted to think back and sentimentalize the past. We yearn for the good old days. People of faith may be especially tempted to engage in such sentimentality, because religious practices and institutions are declining in much of the modern world. In fact, in the early days of Chanukah, some Jews began with eight lit candles and went down to one, because they felt all of Israel's glories were in the past. Once they'd had a powerful united kingdom under Kings David and Solomon. Now they lived under Roman oppression. The light decreased each night to symbolize the decline in Israel's favor in God's eyes.

But one great sage, Rabbi Akiva, prohibited this way of lighting the Chanukah candles. He made it mandatory to begin with one candle and gradually move up to eight. He said God works in history, and while Israel experiences persecution, God ultimately sustains the covenant and will restore them to freedom. Rabbi Akiva said the only way to survive is to look forward without despair, to have faith in the future. His worldview was similar to the one later expressed by Martin Luther King Jr.: "The arc of the moral universe is long but it bends toward justice."[1]

Chanukah is one of the most widely celebrated holidays among American Jews, in part because of its proximity to Christmas. Jews are a tiny minority in America, and since December is a time when many of their neighbors are celebrating a religious holiday, many Jews say it feels right for them to do the same. But American Jews feel a spiritual echo during Chanukah as well. I heard that echo and felt its power in my life one year at a Chanukah party at the White House.

President George W. Bush began the tradition of hosting Jewish leaders from around the country at an annual Chanukah party. My mentor, Rabbi Sam Karff, participated in the first ever White House Chanukah party with President Bush, and I attended an Obama Chanukah party in 2014. Walking in, my wife and I listened to the Marine Band playing the traditional Chanukah song called "Rock of Ages," which praises God's protection of the Jewish people. Then we ate traditional Chanukah foods like fried potato pancakes and donuts. Then the president spoke. In his remarks, President Obama revealed that earlier in the day, he had spoken with a Jewish American named Alan Gross, who had just been released after three years of imprisonment in Cuba. It was one of those extraordinary moments in which God appeared with absolute clarity. Gross's release was not a miracle in the supernatural sense. But to me, it felt like a miracle to be experiencing that holiday at that moment at that place. I realized we were celebrating an individual's return to *freedom* on an ancient holiday celebrating *freedom* in the home of the president of a country built on and dedicated to *freedom*.

Chanukah can feel timeless exactly because its powerful message still resonates in a different time and place. That's one of the reasons the holidays are such a central part of Jewish practice. They add meaning to what we experience and connect us to generations past, present, and future.

PURIM

Another holiday that celebrates the survival of the Jewish people is Purim, for which we move from the ancient temple to Persia, and from the Books of Maccabees to the Book of Esther. The Book of Esther begins with the Persian King Ahasuerus (Xerxes) hosting a six-month drinking feast. When Queen Vashti fails to comply with the king's order to dance for his guests, he has her banished and then begins the search for a new queen. A Jew named Mordecai puts forth his niece Esther as a potential queen, and the king chooses her. He does not know she is Jewish. (This revealing detail in the text helps us put the Book of Esther in historical context. It is set during, and testifies to, a time when many Jews had left the land of Israel and were living in the Diaspora; that is, they were members of a particular nationality living outside of their homeland. Since the text suggests the king did not know Esther was Jewish, we can assume Jews in Persia lived like native Persians. They were acculturated.)

Soon after Esther is made queen, her uncle Mordecai hears of a plot to destroy the Jews of Persia. This plot is the brainchild of the king's advisor, Haman. Haman is the archetypal anti-Semite. He hates the Jews for no apparent reason, and he wants to destroy them completely. Jewish legend suggests Haman is descended from the Amalekite people, who, per the legend, attacked the Israelites in the wilderness without any reason or provocation. As a result, God tells the Israelites to wipe out the name of Amalek from the earth.

I've always understood Amalek as symbolizing pure evil. By commanding the Israelites to wipe out the name of Amalek, God is teaching that one can never compromise with evil. Evil exists. It resists remorse or reconciliation. The only way to respond to evil is to fight it. Mordecai does so when he discovers Haman's plot. He does not urge Esther to try to negotiate with Haman. Rather, Mordecai tells Esther that she must tell the king. The king is the only one who can stop Haman.

Esther initially hesitates. It does not seem to have been typical for a queen to get involved in political affairs in ancient Persia, and, of course, Esther can't be sure how her husband, who still doesn't know she is Jewish, feels about Jews. Seeing her hesitation, Mordecai utters some of the most dramatic words in the Hebrew Bible. He says, "Do not imagine that because you are in the king's palace you alone will escape the fate of all the Jews. For if you remain silent at this time, relief and deliverance for the Jews will arise from another place, but you and your father's house will perish. And who knows if perhaps you have come to the kingdom for such a time as this" (Esther 4:14 BSB).

These words reflect Mordecai's utter confidence that God will ultimately save the Jewish people, and Haman's plan will not be fully realized. Indeed, Mordecai's deep faith is what gives his words such a charge. But God will not save the Jews by sending an angel or by striking Haman dead with a lightning bolt: Mordecai is telling Esther that *she* has the responsibility to serve as God's instrument. She was made queen in order to play a part in the unfolding of God's will.

Ultimately, Esther accedes to Mordecai's request and tells the king of Haman's designs. The king then confronts Haman and quashes his plan. The book ends in a rather gruesome scene where Haman and his family are hung on the gallows Haman had prepared for Mordecai.

Despite the Book of Esther's macabre ending, Purim, the holiday that celebrates Esther's story and the survival of the Persian Jews, is more like a party than the other Jewish holidays. Many Jews wear costumes to the synagogue and act out the Purim story. The Book of Esther itself is also read, and every time the name Haman is read, we make noise with a shaker known as a grogger. By drowning out the hearing of the name of Haman, the descendant of Amalek, the resounding noise of the grogger symbolically fulfills the commandment to blot out the name of Amalek. On Purim we also eat a food known as a *hamentaschen*, which is a pastry made in the shape of a triangular hat. Some scholars suggest Haman wore a similarly shaped triangular hat. The Hebrew word *tasch* also means weaken, so perhaps *hamantaschen* symbolizes the weakening of Haman by God in the Book of Esther.

Purim is also a holiday on which celebrants frequently get drunk. In fact, the Jewish sages say we should become so drunk on Purim that we cannot tell the difference between the names Mordecai and Haman. I have always found this Purim inebriation strange and out of place. Jewish practice rarely embraces the extreme. Alcohol was never forbidden, but its consumption has never been a notable focus—except on Purim. I like to interpret the instruction to drink until one cannot tell the difference between Mordecai and Haman as a call for humility. We often have utter confidence in our opinions. But sometimes we need to see the opposite point of view. Righteousness can descend into self-righteousness. On Purim we enter an upside-down state of mind where we can embrace a different point of view. When we wake up the next morning, perhaps we can act with more civility and respect toward those with whom we disagree.

A less perplexing Purim custom is the delivery of baskets filled with food and other treats known as *mishlach manot*. During Purim we send these baskets of treats to others in the community. We need not give them to close friends; we can give *mishlach manot* to people we occasionally run into. The Purim gift reminds us of the bonds we share. It exemplifies the power of gift-giving to sustain culture. A gift acknowledges our interdependence.

Purim is not just a time of revelry; it is also a day for generosity and community.

PASSOVER

Passover is the holiday that, more than any others, is most likely to be celebrated by American Jews, even those Jews who never go to synagogue. According to scholars, it may be the most ancient continuously observed religious ritual in the Western world.

Passover remains my favorite holiday. Part of the reason Passover resonates for me—and for so many—is its core message. God desires human freedom. God is never on the side of a tyrant. God is always on the side of freedom. This message permeates the entire Passover holiday. Let's see how.

It all begins in Egypt. The first Passover was celebrated on the evening the Israelites left Egypt. The pharaoh of Egypt had relented and allowed them to leave after 230 years of slavery. This release happened only after Moses—who had been raised in Pharaoh's household—returned from exile and followed God's commandment to tell Pharaoh to let the Israelites go free. When Pharaoh initially dismissed Moses, God inflicted ten plagues of increasing severity on Egypt. Finally, after the tenth plague, Pharaoh relented, but only temporarily. He soon changed his mind again and pursued the Israelites. Only when God split open the Red Sea and let the Israelites walk through did they find freedom.

That's the Exodus story in a nutshell. The Passover holiday reflects the way the Jewish people have remembered the Exodus. It centers around a meal. At the center of the meal is a food known as matzah. Matzah is unleavened bread. It is yeast not allowed to rise. While fleeing Egypt, the Israelites did not have time to let their bread rise. They were in a rush because they suspected Pharaoh might change his mind, so they had unleavened bread. We still eat matzah to remember the haste with which they left. And it also reminds us of the experience of slavery. As slaves, the Israelites did not control their time. They could not wait to let their bread rise. The crunchy sound of matzah in our mouths may also recall the whips and lashes the Israelites received as slaves.

Matzah is only one part of the Passover meal. The meal is in fact divided into fifteen sections with accompanying rituals and blessings. This ritual meal is known as a seder, the Hebrew word for "order." The purpose of the rituals is to touch all of our senses and to give participants the experience of the journey from slavery to freedom. In other words, we not only tell the story of the Exodus, we relive it. Near the middle of the seder, all the participants say together "We were slaves. God freed *us* with an outstretched arm." God didn't just deliver our ancestors. God freed us.

The various rituals of the seder reinforce this idea. For example, we take parsley (a symbol of the spring) and dip it in saltwater (a symbol of the tears of slavery). We taste the tears as we eat the parsley. Then we eat a dollop of horseradish, symbolizing the bitterness of slavery. That bitterness is balanced by the sweet charoset—a mixture of apples, nuts, and honey—that represents the mortar the Israelites used to make bricks. Throughout the meal we drink four glasses of wine. Each glass represents one hundred years of the Israelites being "immigrants in a land that isn't their own" (Genesis 15:13). Some Jewish sages also see the four glasses of wine as symbols of the four times the Exodus from Egypt is mentioned in chapter 12 of the Book of Exodus.

If the foods we eat at the seder illustrate the Passover message, so does the story we tell and the way we tell it—the words, but also the dress and the posture of the storytellers. The Jewish sages said every person at a Passover seder should recline in their chairs. During the rabbinic period, reclining at a meal symbolized nobility and freedom. Since Passover is honoring our freedom, and each of us is nobility in the eyes of God, we recline. Some Jewish communities also dress up to reinforce the message. When I studied in Israel, I attended a Passover seder in the home of Yemenite Jews. These were the children and grandchildren of Jewish refugees who had been airlifted out of Yemen in the early 1950s and brought to Israel. Their Passover customs had persisted largely unchanged for at least one thousand years. During their seder, all the men began the evening dressed as Israelite slaves might have been dressed. Before the last glass of wine, they changed into royal garb. Their clothing illustrated the timeless journey from slavery to freedom.

OMER AND SHAVUOT

Passover celebrates freedom. But freedom in Judaism is not an end in itself. It is the prerequisite for responsibility.

Freedom makes it possible for us to choose life, to choose God. The Counting of the Omer symbolizes the journey from slavery to freedom.

The word *omer* denotes a particular measurement: in biblical times, grain was measured by the omer, and this agricultural terminology carried over into Jewish religious practice. Today, instead of counting grain, we count the days between Passover and the next holiday in our cycle, Shavuot (known later in Christianity as Pentecost). Each day we say a blessing with the words "Blessed are you, Eternal God, who sanctifies us with Your Commandments. This is the seventh day of the Omer." We follow this practice until the fiftieth day after Passover, which is the holiday of Shavuot.

The Counting of the Omer has three primary purposes. The first is to be more mindful of the possibilities of each day. Counting time requires us, simply, to make time count. When we say a blessing, we focus our attention. We pause and remind ourselves that this day is a gift from God. This mindfulness is enhanced by a teaching from the Jewish sages. They connected the time between Passover and Shavuot to the time between the Exodus from Egypt and the giving of the Torah to the Israelites at Mount Sinai. For those seven weeks, the Israelites wandered in the wilderness. Would they make it to Sinai? Would they finally be free from the Egyptians? By saying a blessing each day, we remind ourselves of their journey and the faith they had in making it. Some Jews also follow a practice developed by early Jewish mystics. These mystics would focus each day on a different quality or character trait. For example, one day we would try to be especially mindful of humility and study a few texts related to it. Another day we might focus on charity or peace. Each day invites us to deepen a virtue.

The Counting of the Omer also helps us understand the meaning of freedom. The essence of freedom is control over our time. It's ours to count, not someone else's to control. And we make time count by pursuing meaningful actions. One of my practices is to study my favorite book of the Talmud every day during the Counting of the Omer. The book is called *Pirke Avot*, "Ethics of the Ancestors." It is a collection of rabbinic aphorisms and wisdom, and I think of it as the greatest self-help book ever written. Its most famous teaching might be "If I am not for myself, who will be for me? If I am only for myself, what am I? And if not now, when?" This saying gives us a framework for making decisions. We have to provide for, protect, and stand up for ourselves. God built us as individuals with free will. Yet, our lives lack meaning if we do not live for something bigger than ourselves. And our time on earth is limited. We keep all these truths in mind when we make decisions, and a life of freedom requires us to make meaningful choices.

Finally, Counting the Omer helps us prepare for Shavuot. The word *shavuot* means weeks. It is derived from the Hebrew letters *shin-vet-ayin*, which are understood to together indicate the number seven. A week is seven days, and Shavuot is the holiday that comes after seven weeks. It is the fiftieth day after the Counting of the Omer.

Originally, Shavuot occurred at harvest time. But the Jewish sages transformed this agricultural holiday into a spiritual one celebrating the giving of the Torah. We might say the Torah is the ultimate harvest of divine wisdom. It nourishes our spirit like bread nourishes our body.

YOM HAZIKARON
AND YOM HAATZMAUT

These two holidays are the most recent additions to the Jewish calendar. They began in the state of Israel as a way of honoring the dead who died in Israel's wars and celebrating the date Israel became a recognized sovereign state. They are celebrated one after the other, with Memorial Day on fourth day of the Hebrew Month of Iyar, and Independence Day on the fifth day of Iyar. These days usually fall in April or May.

In the United States, where today the majority of citizens do not serve in active-duty military service, Memorial Day is often thought of as just part of a three-day weekend. But in Israel, almost every family has someone in the service. Israel has fought six wars in its seventy years. Three years of military service is mandatory for almost every male beginning at age eighteen, and two and a half years are required for women. In America about 7.6 percent of the population has served in the military at one point in their lives.[2] In Israel about 80 percent have served; army service is a pervasive and visible part of the culture. Every high school has a corner devoted to students who died in Israel's wars. Every family has lost or has known people who died in war. Memorial Day has personal meaning for virtually every Israeli.

Yom HaAtzmaut celebrates the day Israel became a state. On May 14, 1948, which corresponds to the fifth day of the Hebrew month of Iyar, the provisional government of Israel signed and recited Israel's Declaration of Independence. Israelis celebrate the holidays with parades and hikes, and many army bases open up to allow visitors. The transition between Memorial Day and Independence Day begins at sundown on the fourth of Iyar with the raising of the Israeli flag from half-staff to the top of the flagpole. This ceremony takes place atop Mount Herzl in Jerusalem and is followed by a parade of the flags of the each of major military divisions. In synagogues in Israel and around the world, many Jews recite a series of psalms called Hallel, which means "praise." (It comes from the same Hebrew root as the word *Halleluyah*). At my synagogue we also sing the Israeli national anthem, "HaTikvah," which means "the hope."

The observances of these two holidays illustrate an important part of Jewish identity—belonging is as important as believing. Our religious self-understanding is derived from our sense of communal identity as well as our beliefs about God.

TISHA B'AV

The last holiday in the Jewish year is not a celebration but a day of mourning: Tisha B'Av. (The name simply means the ninth day of the month of Av). On Tisha B'Av, Jews mourn several calamitous events in Jewish history that happened on the ninth of Av. The first temple—constructed by King Solomon as described in the Bible—was destroyed by the Babylonians on the ninth of Av. According to Jewish legend, the second temple was also destroyed on the ninth of Av in 70 CE. Some scholars even speculate that the leaders of the Spanish Inquisition chose the ninth of Av as the date for the expulsion of Jews from Spain as a way of making it even more miserable. Incidentally, Christopher Columbus's ship was delayed from leaving the harbor for three days around the ninth of Av in 1492 because so many Jews were leaving at the same time.

Tisha B'Av is typically observed by fasting and by the public reading of the biblical Book of Lamentations. The lights of the synagogue are dimmed. A mood of sorrow abounds.

But not all Jews observe the ninth of Av as solely a day of mourning. Some see it as a sign of fulfillment of God's mission for the Jews. In the mid-nineteenth century, led by a liberal theologian named Samuel Holdheim, several rabbis said the destruction of the first and second temples—which were the primary reasons for the mourning on the ninth of Av—were actually positive events in Jewish history because they brought Jews out of the land of Israel and into the wider world. Had Jews remained in the land, Judaism might have evolved into more of a nationalism—a race and an ethnicity—than a world-transforming faith. By leaving the land, Jews brought the message of monotheism to the world. In other words, the destruction of the temple enabled the rise of a more universalist Judaism. In addition, had the temple not been destroyed and Jews remained centered in the land of Israel, they may have been conquered by other nations and lost to history.

This interpretation is not the only way modern rabbis have sought to connect Tisha B'Av to the present. In 2016, I was invited to speak to a multi-synagogue gathering on Tisha B'av. That year Tisha B'av fell in August, in the midst of a heated and divisive presidential election. The audience to which I was speaking was strongly divided, politically and religiously. They included Orthodox and Reform Jews, and Republicans and Democrats. I looked to the lessons of this holy day for insights into how we can navigate through today's conflicts. That is one of the core reasons we study God's Word and observe holidays. We have faith that the past, present, and future are connected, and that God's Word transcends time and space.

I found what I was looking for a story from the Talmud. It uses a parable to explain why God allowed the temple to be destroyed by the Romans. The parable begins with a man named Kamza, who throws a party. He invites everyone to the party except his enemy, whose name is Bar Kamza. Bar Kamza is embarrassed not to be invited, so he implores Kamza to invite him. When Kamza refuses, Bar Kamza offers to pay for the catering. Kamza refuses. Then Bar Kamza offers to pay for half of the costs of the party—half of the food, half of the entertainment, half of the flowers. Kamza still refuses. Ultimately, Bar Kamza does not attend. He is angry not only at Kamza but also at the rabbis who attended Kamza's party and refused to rebuke him for inviting everybody but Bar Kamza. They refused to seek shalom, peace, in the community.

Bar Kamza's anger at his community—which he sees as rejecting him—leads him to create a blemish on a sacrificial offering made at the temple in honor of the Roman emperor. When the emperor hears about the blemished offering, he becomes angry at the perceived lack of respect given to him by the Jews, and sends in his troops to destroy them and the temple.

The story of Kamza and Bar Kamza is not meant to be taken as actual history. Rather, it is a parable that reveals the divisions in the Jewish community in the first century of the Common Era, and the horrific consequences those divisions entailed. Two people—whose similar names are meant to suggest their familial and tribal connection—cannot find a way to coexist. Kamza's hatred for Bar Kamza is so great that he will not make any accommodation to save him from embarrassment. Bar Kamza's pride and anger are so great that he is willing to expose his fellow Jews to the ire of the Roman Empire because of the way he was treated. And moral leaders of the people—the rabbis—lack the courage to stand up for the unity of the community, as illustrated in their participation in Kamza's party even as they knew he refused to invite Bar Kamza. The community's divisions—and lack of wise leadership—led to its destruction.

In speaking about the parable to the multi-synagogue audience, I highlighted the way this kind of hatred and lack of civility was spreading today. The refusal of people from one political party or religious group to talk with another had become commonplace. Engagements were breaking up over support for competing candidates. Respected intellectuals were predicting a potential civil war in America. The story of Kamza and Bar Kamza serves as a warning. If we do not find a way to be civil—to disagree while maintaining relationships and mutual respect—we risk self-destruction. The solution is not to give up what we believe. Rather, it is to not let political beliefs define us and our relationships.

We Americans cannot let our partisan identities become so defining that they prevent us from acknowledging and associating with people with other points of view. Jews cannot let our particular approach to Jewish practice become a wall that cuts us off from others. Each of us—whatever our faith or nationality—can focus on our similarities rather than our differences. And leaders should aim for achieving shalom—peace—rather than fanning the flames of division. Leaders who encourage conflict resemble Bar Kamza, who fomented tension between the Roman Empire and the Jewish community. His embarrassment led to anger, which led to destruction. A wise leader, in contrast, seeks ways to forgive and repair.

FAITH IN THE FUTURE

Even though Tisha B'Av is a time of sorrow and lament, it lasts only for one day only; we cannot forget the past but neither can we dwell in it. Shortly after Tisha B'Av, the annual holiday cycle begins again with the Jewish New Year, Rosh Hashanah. The eating of apples and honey on Rosh Hashanah symbolizes the hopes for sweetness and joy in the new year.

7

PRAYER

Experiencing Oneness

E very year at my synagogue we host an interfaith Passover seder attended by groups from various churches and seminaries. The first year we hosted it, an elderly gentleman asked a question. He began by apologizing if the question sounded naive or rude. Then he asked, "What about the Passover sacrifice?" A few people gasped at the question. Was he suggesting that we perform an animal sacrifice?

I responded by assuring him it was not a rude or naive question nor was it an unfamiliar question. Because some people mistakenly believe that sacrificial offering is a part of Jewish ritual, I've been asked similar questions before. The Torah, after all, devotes significant attention to ritual sacrifice, which was the primary method of worship in ancient times. Significant sections of Exodus, Numbers, and Leviticus describe sacrificial practices in detail, so I am not shocked or offended if people wonder about the existence of animal sacrifice; they are simply asking about something they've read a lot about in their Bible.

I explain that the practice of animal sacrifice ended almost two thousand years ago, when the second temple in Jerusalem was destroyed by the Romans. Prayers (offerings of the heart) replaced sacrifices (offerings of the hands). The rabbis who developed the Jewish liturgy—the prescribed order of offering daily, sabbath, and holiday prayers—modeled the timing and purpose of prayer on the sacrificial system. For example, Jews pray three times a day, corresponding to the morning, afternoon, and evening sacrifices described in the Bible. An additional worship service is conducted on sabbath morning, just as an additional sacrifice was offered on the sabbath morning. Even the terminology of prayer and sacrifice mirror each other. One of the Hebrew words for sacrifice is *avodah*. One of the Hebrew words for prayer is also *avodah*.

To be sure, verbal prayer was not brand-new; it had coexisted with sacrifices. Jesus prayed from the Psalter, and in the Hebrew Bible we see Hannah praying with words. But before the destruction of the Jerusalem temple, sacrificial offerings served as primary way of communing with God. After its destruction, verbal prayer became central to Jewish worship.

This chapter examines the way Jews pray and how contemporary Jewish prayer came to be. We look at the transition from sacrifice to prayer, the emergence of the Jewish prayer book, and some of the differences in Jewish prayer practices today. We will also consider the similarities and differences between Christian churches and Jewish synagogues.

OUT OF THE ASHES

In the first century of the Common Era, Judaism almost died. After a vicious war with the Romans, the Jewish people saw their temple destroyed. Tens of thousands of people—including many of the Sadducees, one of the important Jewish communities during the era of Jesus— were killed. Some survivors fled to the caves by the Dead

Sea and developed their own sect. Others joined the growing movement of Jesus followers, not yet known as Christianity.

The only group of Jewish leaders with sufficient numbers and authority to lead the Jewish people after the massive Roman defeat was the Pharisees. They had survived by advocating negotiations with the Romans, and they had earned the trust of the people through their teachings and piety. Ultimately, the Pharisees became known as the rabbis—a title meaning "teacher"—and by 100 CE, their teachings governed the remaining Jewish community.

One of the most pressing tasks for the Pharisees was to develop a system of worship that could be sustained outside the temple. With no temple, how were people to connect with and offer themselves to God? The Torah consistently says that sacrificial offerings can only be made in the temple. Thus, sacrificial offerings were no longer an option. In order to substitute for those sacrifices, the rabbis crafted a system of verbal prayers and modeled the timing and format of those prayers on the sacrificial system.

The first prayer services probably centered around communal meals at the rabbis' homes. Over time these gathering places became larger and more formalized. They are the prototype of what we now call synagogues. The earliest synagogues were built in Greece and North Africa well before the temple was destroyed. They were the places where Jews who lived outside of the land of Israel and Jerusalem would gather. They may have gathered for prayer or just for communal solidarity. In Alexandria, Egypt, for example, new arrivals in town would come to the synagogue to find work. You could meet fellow shoemakers or blacksmiths or most other trades by going into their particular section in the synagogue. The synagogue was not just a house of worship, it was also a community center that not only included space for worship but also became a place to meet other community needs.

After the destruction of the temple, the rabbis established more places where the community could gather, meet together, and pray. These were not always freestanding structures. Some community gatherings took place in people's homes. Others groups convened in schools. The people mattered more than the building. This view reflected in the exhortation in Exodus 25:8 where God says, "Build me a sanctuary so that I may dwell among *them*" (author's translation). The Bible does not say God dwells in the sanctuary. God does not reside in the building. Rather, God dwells *among* the people.

MINYAN

To this end, one of the early requirements the rabbis introduced into prayer services is the *minyan*. A minyan is a quorum. Specifically, it is the ritual gathering of ten or more people. A minyan is required in order for the full Jewish prayer service to be recited. Anyone can pray alone or in a smaller group, but the rabbis designated certain prayers for communal prayer only. This had two effects: first, it helped keep Jewish communities together—if you wanted to pray with other Jews three times a day, you'd likely, by default, live and work near other Jews. Second, it encoded in Judaism the sense that prayer is about both the individual person speaking from the depths of the person's soul to

God *and* the community speaking from the depths of its collective identity to the God who made them a holy nation. Indeed, prayer in Judaism is intensely communal. It is as much about sociology as it is about theology. One Talmudic verse even says God hears the prayers of a community more clearly than God hears the prayers of an individual.

Initially, I was troubled by this teaching. Why would God care if we prayed around other people? But the obligation to support another person often pushes us to do things we may not otherwise do. Many people who are trying to exercise will commit to a running group or even just meeting a friend at the gym to work out together in the morning. If you do not show up, you leave your friend alone on his treadmill. The fact that you know he'll be expecting you pushes you to show up. The same is true in prayer. People show up because others in the minyan are counting on them. If they don't come, the others may not be able to form a minyan, and certain prayers won't be prayed. But the power of group prayer goes even deeper. Sometimes we are made more aware of our own capacities and yearnings by the presence of others. We realize our capacity to comfort others when one of our fellow pray-ers is in mourning. We experience shared joy when we see a child learn and lead worship even if the child is not our own. I like to think of communal prayer as positive peer pressure. It brings out our best qualities and inclinations and deepens our connections with others. The rabbis' psychological astuteness helped keep the Jewish people connected to one another in the aftermath of the destruction of the temple.

TORAH READING

Another core practice of Jewish prayer is a reading of a section of the Torah scroll. The Torah scroll is made out of lambskin and written by hand. The reader is known as a *ba-al kriya*. In ancient times, the Torah was typically read on Mondays, Thursdays, and Saturday mornings. Mondays and Thursdays were market days, and the rabbis likely concluded that more people would be present then. Saturday is the sabbath day when attendance was likely the largest. The readers likely followed the traditional division in which the Torah is divided into fifty-four sections, and with a few variations, the entire scroll would be read in one year. At the end of the weekly reading, the Torah reader typically lifts the Torah scroll to show the congregation God's Word. Scholars speculate that this practice originated to ensure the people that they were hearing God's true Word, and not the words of a false or different scroll.

CENTRAL PRAYERS:
SHEMA AND KADDISH

Today, Jewish prayer services include many prayers of varying lengths. Several are especially treasured by Jews around the world. One of these is the Shema, words from Deuteronomy 6 that declare God's oneness. The twice-daily recitation of Deuteronomy 6 had become a core part of Jewish worship by the beginning of the Common Era; perhaps, speculate some scholars, during the era when the temple still stood, sacrificial offerings were accompanied by short blessings or recitations that may have evolved into prayers when sacrifices were no longer offered. If indeed recitation of Scripture verses accompanied temple sacrifices, the Shema was likely included.

Even today many rabbis refer to the Shema as the watchword of the Jewish faith. The Shema also serves as a form of last rites. When I visit someone in the hospital, we often recite the Shema together if possible. During the Holocaust, some recited it as they died in the gas chamber— affirming their faith at a harrowing time.

Another core prayer of this era is the kaddish. Scholars believe the kaddish is among Judaism's most ancient formal prayers because it contains several Aramaic words. Aramaic was spoken across the ancient Near East shortly before and after the beginning of the Common Era. The rhythm and message of the kaddish also mirror the Lord's Prayer. Both extol God's name and sovereignty. Both invoke God as *father*. Both envision a better world of divine perfection. Today both are often recited at funerals and most worship services.

The kaddish is the primary Jewish prayer of mourning. It is recited at the graveside right after burial. It is then recited twice a day for eleven months after the burial by a spouse or child who is in mourning. Every year, on the anniversary of a loved one's death, family members will come to the synagogue to say the kaddish. Notably, the prayer itself does not express mournful sentiments: it praises God and articulates wishes for peace. Some mourners have said they appreciate that the requisite mourner's prayer says nothing about grief exactly because they, the mourners, need liturgies to help them continue to praise God from the depths of despair.

The kaddish is one of the prayers that can be recited in a minyan. Some people come to corporate worship just to be there for others who want to say kaddish. They commit themselves to attending worship as part of a minyan to support spouses or children who are saying kaddish, hoping that others would do the same for them if the need should arise. Like the Shema, the kaddish is a prayer many Jews know. I have seen people who have not attended worship services in decades somehow remember the words of the kaddish at a loved one's funeral.

The kaddish, however, did not begin as a prayer of mourning. It originated in schools. After a teacher would deliver a lecture, the students would rise in unison and recite the kaddish. The teacher was helping the students to understand God's Word, and the students responded to honor the teacher by praising God's name. When a leading teacher or rabbi died, the students would gather at his home, and the rabbi's son would lead a study session that would also end with the recitation of the kaddish in his honor. Thus, the prayer became one that both honored a living teacher and a teacher who had died. The kaddish became more intimately linked with mourning during the Crusades, when Jewish towns were decimated by crusaders traveling through Europe on their way to the Holy Land. Survivors of the Crusades began lighting a candle and reciting the names of their loved ones on the anniversaries of their deaths. Since leading rabbis were among the many murdered, mourners recited the kaddish prayer. Soon it became inextricably connected to mourning.

Like the Lord's Prayer, the kaddish moves worshippers deeply, and in often unexpected ways. At my synagogue, we say the kaddish at the end of every worship service. I read the names of those who have died during the last thirty days. Before the kaddish, I also read the names of those who died during this week in years past. Many members of my synagogue who do not worship regularly do come to synagogue to say kaddish on the anniversary of a loved one's death. This date is known as *yahrzeit*. One year a synagogue member I did not know well came for *yahrzeit*. I read through the list of kaddish names—which the synagogue office prepares for me using a database on our computer system—as usual. I returned to my study after the worship service and prepared to go home.

As I was leaving, this synagogue member walked briskly through the open door of my study. A look of both anger and despair was on her face. She began speaking to me in a tone usually reserved for airport workers when a flight is severely delayed. She demanded to know why I did not read her father's name. She said I was disrespecting his memory. He would be rolling over in his grave, she said, because of what I had done. She even said she wasn't sure if Judaism mattered to her at all anymore.

I was taken aback. Her father's name was not on the kaddish list. She had never informed the synagogue of his death, which had occurred fourteen years ago. But the pain of loss—and missing an opportunity to acknowledge that loss in this most central prayer—hurt my congregant at her core. Even though I didn't feel directly at fault for the omission of her father, I apologized and invited her to come back with me into the sanctuary. We stood in front of the ark (the sacred place where the Torah is housed). I gave her a Torah to hold, I recited her father's name, and together we said the kaddish prayer. Tears streamed down her face. It was one of those moments where prayer enters into what Rabbi Joshua Heschel calls "the ineffable." As a rabbi I felt the truth of a phrase from the Talmud—"For this moment, you were created." *I was created to be a rabbi for that moment of healing.* That moment also taught me the power of prayer. It creates a space for us to communicate with and experience God.

Prayer can also touch our deepest selves. One of the Hebrew words connected to prayer is *li-heet-palel.* It means "to pray." It is also what grammarians call a reflexive verb. That means the direct object of the verb is also the subject of the verb. For example, in the sentence, "I wash myself," the word *wash* is functioning as a reflexive verb. The subject and object are the same.

Because *li-heet-palel* is a reflexive verb, the pray-er is both the subject and the object of the verb *to pray.* That seems strange. Shouldn't God be the object of our prayers? Are we supposed to pray to ourselves? No, we are not. But prayer in Judaism is more than saying words to and about God. The Hebrew letters pey-lamed-lamed, which make the up the root letters of the word *li-heet-palel* are also the root letters of the verb *to judge.* In other words, when we pray, we are judging ourselves. We are looking inward to see if we are the person we are meant to be. But that is not all. What does a judge do? A judge looks at all the evidence. A judge looks and weighs our actions and attributes. A judge seeks to find the truth. When we pray, we look for that truth within us. We look at our whole character. And the Torah teaches that God is a merciful Judge. So we are to be merciful with ourselves. Prayer invites us to look at ourselves but also to have compassion on ourselves. Prayer makes that process a vital part of our lives.

PRAYER BOOKS

As we have noted, there was some spoken prayer when the temple stood; after it was destroyed, the rabbis began systematizing prayer, deciding what times of the day prayers were to be said. Then, around the ninth century, leading rabbis created a fixed order of prayer. They organized the prayer service to ensure certain prayers the rabbis deemed important were always said. A rabbi named Saadia Gaon compiled the first order of prayer. His book included the prayers he believed were important and the order in which they should be recited. Scholars do not know how widespread Saadia Gaon's prayer book was when he compiled it, but over time, it became the foundation of the prayer book we still use today.

The prayer book seeks to evoke a spiritual journey. It begins with prayers of gratitude that cultivate a feeling of thanks toward God. It continues with the recitation of biblical and talmudic texts. Most of these texts reflect core Jewish values and beliefs. They serve as a "greatest hits" of Jewish wisdom. Then we have more prayers of gratitude, most of which are phrased as blessings. (Blessings begin with the words "Blessed are you, Eternal God, Sovereign of the Universe.")

After the opening blessings of gratitude and recitation of texts, we move to a section called "The Shema and Its Blessings." This section steps up the intensity— it's as if we have warmed up and are getting into the spiritual workout.

Many of these prayers are call and response. The prayer leader sings a line, and the worshippers respond in unison. The central prayer in this section is the Shema, which, as we noted earlier, is the watchword of the Jewish faith. It affirms God's oneness with a verse from Deuteronomy. This verse is often said softly with our eyes closed. Many worshippers stand up as they say it. Standing is a sign of respect and awe for God. Closing our eyes is a form of concentration. We are focusing on the words themselves without any distractions. Prayer is an act of listening to God's words as we say them, and the Shema underscores this listening, as its first word, *shema*, means "listen!" We do not experience God through icons or imagery. We hear God through spoken words. And God hears us. That's one of the truths about prayer. God is always available to listen even when other people are not.

AMIDAH

Following the Shema and its surrounding blessings, we come to the central part of the worship service known as the Amidah. The word *amidah* means "standing," and throughout the recitation of the Amidah section of worship, we stand. The Amidah section is filled with petitionary prayers, prayers that ask God for things: redemption, sustenance, return from exile, and so on. Most of the prayers of petition fall in the Amidah section. On every day except the sabbath, the amidah includes nineteen short prayers. On the sabbath, however, almost all the petitionary prayers are removed because the sabbath is a day to thank and appreciate rather than request things from God.

We also frequently adapt and make additions to the Amidah prayers to reflect a particular season or holiday. For example, during the summer and spring months, we ask God to provide wind and rain. In the winter and fall, we ask God to provide dew. On several holidays, we insert prayers of petition or thanksgiving asking or thanking God for something connected to the holiday. On Rosh Hashanah and Yom Kippur, for example, we ask God to "inscribe us for life in the book of life." During Chanukah, we insert a special blessing thanking God for all the miracles of ages past. All these prayers are placed inside the Amidah.

Near the end, the Amidah also provides a space for us to pray silently. When leading worship, I often invite people to pray for what they seek in their lives. Silent prayer is the time when a fixed liturgy gives us an opportunity for spontaneous, real-time reflection. Over the course of my ministry, I have noticed more and more people request greater time for silent prayer. At least a few times a year, someone writes me an email asking if I could allow a little more time for it. I have also noticed more people closing their eyes during silent prayer and looking focused. This focus is in sharp contrast to what I noticed around me growing up, when most of the adults seemed to either look around the sanctuary or whisper something to their neighbor during silent prayer. Perhaps this reflects the need for private silent places in an increasingly noisy culture.

It also reflects a deeper appreciation today in Judaism of spontaneous personal prayer. As we have noted, Jewish prayer rests on a fixed liturgy. The order of prayers today follows what was established 1,100 years ago. Aside from the time for silent prayer, for which some synagogues only allot a few seconds, Jewish prayer is highly structured. This fixed structure did not arise out of a rabbinic aversion to private prayer. Rather, it reflects the way the ancient rabbis thought about the *role* of prayer in Judaism.

In Judaism, praying the liturgy is first and foremost the fulfillment of a legal requirement. It is not primarily a means to a spiritual experience. It is not primarily a chance to talk with God. It is a fulfillment of our obligations. Those obligations are outlined in the Torah. They are elaborated upon and further specified in the Talmud. And we meet our obligations when we gather in a minyan and follow the liturgy.

What this means in practice is that a Jewish worship service may feel rote and inaccessible to someone who is not familiar with the liturgy. The primarily point for many pray-ers is simply to say the prayers. If one feels close to God while doing so, wonderful, but that's not the driving purpose. Fulfilling our obligation to God is.

In this way, when I have attended a Catholic or Eastern Orthodox church, I feel a sense of familiarity. I know that, in part, people are there because it is a fundamental obligation of Catholic or Orthodox life to participate in certain corporate liturgies. I know that some people in the church feel spiritually engaged, and others probably do not. This is not how I have always felt at Protestant churches, which seem to me to be characterized by more spontaneous prayer and more public emotion; there, it seems to me that the emphasis is perhaps less on obligation and more on feeling. I am only a guest in these Christian services, of course, and I may be misperceiving them, but fundamentally I have been struck by the great range of church worship services—

Catholic liturgy that feels somewhat familiar to me, silent Quaker worship that feels beautiful but very different from Jewish worship, and everything in between.

ACTION AS PRAYER

As I just mentioned, Quaker corporate worship involves a lot of silence. A Quaker friend with whom I spoke about the experience of Quaker silence pointed out to me that silence is not the only way Quakers pray. Quakers also consider their pursuits of a just and peaceful world prayer. This is true for Jews too. Not all prayer consists of words. One of the great Jewish theologians of the twentieth century was a rabbi named Abraham Joshua Heschel. Heschel was born in Warsaw, Poland, near the beginning of the twentieth century. He came from a long line of distinguished rabbis. But the world around him was changing, and Heschel was the first of his family to attend a secular university. He wrote poetry and studied the classics of Western literature. He remained, however, a devout and faithful Jew.

When the Nazis came to power in 1933, Heschel was living in Germany. Unable to find work commensurate with his learning, to make ends meet, he began teaching Jewish prayer and philosophy at a groundbreaking school of adult Jewish learning. As the Nazi persecution of Jews grew more intense, Heschel searched for a way out. In 1940, as the Nazis invaded much of Western Europe, he was able to leave Germany on a special religious scholars visa. He became a professor at the Hebrew Union College in Cincinnati, the rabbinical seminary for Reform rabbis (which I attended). Soon he moved to New York to teach at the Jewish Theological Seminary, which trains Conservative rabbis. He taught Jewish ethics and mysticism. The study of Jewish mysticism—which we will touch on in chapter 10— focuses on the hidden meanings and message of the Torah.

Heschel's view of prayer reflected his passion and mystical sensibility. The week after the voting rights march in Selma, Alabama—the famous march over the Edmund Pettis Bridge—one of Heschel's student asked him why he'd participated in the march. Heschel responded, "I was praying with my feet." Prayer is not only talking with God. It is the way God speaks to our highest selves. It is a way of connecting our inner life and our outer world.

SHABBAT

The core of Jewish prayer is Shabbat, the sabbath. Shabbat begins shortly before sundown on Friday evening and ends just after sunset on Saturday night. Shabbat involves prayer, study, and rest. Many Jews do not work or spend money on the sabbath. There are actually thirty-nine categories of work forbidden on the sabbath. They are derived from the thirty-nine types of work the Israelites did in creating the portable tabernacle in the wilderness in the Book of Exodus, activities from which they rested on the sabbath. The forbidden work falls broadly into the categories of producing and creating. That means no cooking, writing, or snapping on a lamp to light up a dark room. In the words of Rabbi Joseph Soloveitchik, on Shabbat, we appreciate rather than create.[1]

Even though most twenty-first-century Jews do not follow
all the traditional laws of the sabbath, they do recognize
that Shabbat keeps us connected to one another and to God.
In other words, even those Jews who do not pray or study
on the sabbath know that the time from Friday sundown to
Saturday sundown is Shabbat. Imagine people who choose
not to drink champagne or visit Time's Square on New
Year's Eve: they may not be doing the stereotypical things
many Americans do for New Year's, but they likely still
know that it is New Year's Eve. The sabbath is similar for
most Jews. They may not be attending synagogue or having
a special dinner at their homes. But most know it is Shabbat.
They recognize life should not be all about creating and
producing. We need to take time for rest and appreciation.

Many of the prayers Jews say on Shabbat—the kaddish,
the Shema—we also say during the week. But Shabbat prayer
has one distinction, a distinct *omission*. Jewish prayer falls
into three types: prayers of gratitude, of petition, and of
praise. Prayers of gratitude thank God for things like our
health and our safety. Prayers of praise laud God's attributes.
Prayers of petition make requests of God. A typical daily
prayer service mixes the three. We ask God for wisdom. We
praise God's mercy. We thank God for our bodies.

On Shabbat, as noted above, we offer no prayers of
petition. We do not ask God for anything because Shabbat is
a time of appreciation. Instead of constantly wanting more,
we find joy and fullness in what we have. One Christian
minister gave me one of the best descriptions of Shabbat
when he said that it's a time not for wishing but for savoring.
During the week, we can wish and work. On Shabbat, we
savor the world as it is.

There is, however, one exception to the rule of no prayers of petition on Shabbat. We still say a prayer asking for peace. Peace—the Hebrew word is *shalom*—is such a high value in Judaism that we beseech God for it even on Shabbat. When we say the prayer for peace, we actually move our bodies, taking three steps back. One of the interpretations of this practice is that in order to make peace, we have to make space for someone else. In prayer, we try to give up some of ourselves to God. Ultimately, we come out strengthened. Similarly, we have to give up a little bit of ourselves to make space for others. Ultimately, the space we create for others makes a more peaceful world more possible for us all.

We pray for peace on Shabbat in the synagogue. But peace begins in the home. So next we will examine the central roles the home and synagogue play in Jewish life.

~~~~~~~~~

8

Everyday Holiness

Homes, Food, Blessings

~~~~~~~~~

One of the most influential rabbis in America is a man named Abraham Twerski. I have a special fondness for his work because, like me, he grew up in Milwaukee and, like me, he has a deep interest in the connection between psychology and spirituality. Rabbi Twerski has worked with Alcoholics Anonymous and partnered with leading physicians and scientists in exploring the role of spirituality and faith in overcoming addictions. He has also written about the role of faith in building self-esteem and instilling a sense of personal responsibility.

I enjoy all of Rabbi Twerski's writing, but I especially love his descriptions of his childhood. He was born into a prominent and distinguished rabbinical family. His parents, grandparents, great-grandparents, and ancestors were famous rabbis. One of his cousins founded the Jewish Studies program at Harvard. He lived with high parental expectations. Like many, he struggled with them. But he found comfort in the Jewish rituals observed in his home.

Rabbi Twerski describes the way his family observed Shabbat in the home. His mom would light the two sabbath candles. Lighting those candles and saying the accompanying blessings is part of the standard sabbath ritual. But then his mom would light another set of candles for each child in the family. He had four brothers, so the house was filled with six sets of candles. This candle-lighting happened every sabbath evening.[1]

As he grew up, Rabbi Twerski thought back to those evenings. He thought back to the set of candles lit for each child and realized that his life—the simple fact that he was born—brought light into the world. That knowledge helped him through difficult times and helped him see the power of religious rituals we practice in the home.

THE HOME

In Judaism, the home is the central site of religious life, marking a key difference between Judaism and Christianity. For many Christians, the geographical center of Christian life is the church. Attendance at church is a key marker of religious commitment. Many churches judge their strength by the number of worshippers who come on Sunday morning. While the synagogue is critically important in Judaism, the home is more so. Preparing and sharing a Shabbat dinner at home is every bit as much an expression of devotion as praying at a synagogue; and it may be that more Jews make a special Friday night dinner than attend Friday night services at synagogue. One mystical Jewish teaching says that the messiah will only come when the sabbath is perfectly observed in every Jewish home.

The home was not always the center of Jewish religious life. Before 70 CE, the Jerusalem temple was central. The temple was the place where God resided. The temple was the place where, in a beautiful Talmudic phrase, heaven and earth touched. But when the Romans destroyed the temple, the meeting point between heaven and earth shifted. No longer did we commune with God in a great temple.

Rather, every home became a temple. The Jewish sages called the home a *mikdash me-at*, a miniature temple. The dining table replaced the altar. The words we exchanged with one another across the table and the songs we sang on Friday nights over dessert replaced the animal sacrifices. A mezuzah—an artistic vessel containing snippets from the Torah—was placed on the doorposts of the home, marking it as a sacred space. Mezuzahs remain a reminder of the imperative to behave with holiness in our homes. Some Jews place a mezuzah on the doorposts of every room in their home. The mezuzahs hang upward and diagonally toward the room. This way of hanging a mezuzah comes out of a debate between two rabbis, Hillel and Shammai. One said the mezuzah should hang vertically, pointing up toward heaven. He reasoned that the mezuzah reminded us of God's presence in the home. The other said it should hang horizontally, pointing into the room. He reasoned that the mezuzah should remind us to bring sacredness *into the room*. Ultimately, they compromised, so today mezuzahs hang diagonally. Perhaps that is a reminder that *shalom bayit*, peace in the home, depends on compromise.

The home remains a sacred center of contemporary Jewish life. We see this most vividly in the realms of food and blessings. Both attempt to infuse holiness and a sense of the sacred into ordinary daily life.

YOU ARE WHAT YOU EAT?

Have you ever been to a restaurant and noticed someone taking a picture of their meal? The first time I saw this happen I asked the server if something had gone wrong with the meal. No, she said, the couple was just documenting the meal for Instagram. It turns out food aficionados are an enormous presence on Instagram, and part of the reason we like to follow Instagram foodies is that they elevate eating into something more than simply giving nutrition to our bodies. Meals become an aesthetic, meaningful experience.

For Jews, eating has always been more than a way of getting nutrition. It has been an ethical, holy experience. That is the purpose of the laws known as *kashrut*, more commonly known as keeping kosher.

You have probably heard of kosher food. Perhaps you have bought kosher pickles or a kosher turkey at the supermarket. Kosher foods are those prepared according to Jewish dietary laws. Among other things, these laws define the proper way to slaughter animals and prepare meats; the types of meats permitted; and what foods can be served and prepared with one another. For example, dairy foods and meat dishes cannot be served together. In other words, kosher laws do not permit cheeseburgers.

The dietary laws are derived from the Bible and elaborated upon in the Talmud. The law of not mixing milk and meat, for example, is derived from a verse in the Book of Leviticus forbidding the boiling of a calf in its mother's milk. So, if you refuse ever to mix meat and milk in the kitchen, you are certain never to boil a calf in its mother's milk. This restriction may seem extreme, but it reflects a Jewish principle known as "building a fence around the Torah." We place additional restrictions to ensure we do not violate God's Word. It is like visiting a museum and approaching a famous painting. A rope in front of the painting will stop us from getting too close to the painting in order to ensure that we do not touch it. In theory nothing is wrong with walking close to the painting. But the closer we walk to it, the higher the risk is that we touch it. To ensure that never happens, the museum forbids us from walking too close. When it comes to God's laws, we want to be sure we do not violate them. Therefore, we establish additional restrictions to ensure we do not.

But Jewish dietary practices in the home are not simply about restrictions. They reflect a desire for holiness. In modern English, the word *holy* is synonymous with adjectives like *awesome* or *sacred*. But in biblical Hebrew, the word *holy*—which is *kadosh*—has a slightly different meaning. *Kadosh* means separate, or separated, or set apart: to be holy is to be different. It is to be separate and set apart for a divine purpose. The sabbath day, for example, is set apart from the other days of the week. The land of Israel is set apart from the other nations of world. Even the Hebrew word for a marriage—*kiddushin*—is derived from the word *kadosh*, suggesting the idea that holy matrimony describes a relationship in which the bride and groom are "set apart" for one another. In the spiritual life, we do not always know exactly for what purpose we've been set aside; sometimes God has hidden that knowledge from us. But we trust that if we are set apart—on Shabbat, from the bustle of the week; in our marriages, from intimate love with people not our spouse—we will have the space and focus to discover that purpose.

By eating only kosher foods, we are turning eating into a holy act in both the *way* we eat and the *types of foods* we eat. Instead of being merely a way to fuel our bodies, eating becomes a way of approaching God.

WHY SO MANY LAWS?

In the Gospel of Matthew, Jesus says "What goes into someone's mouth does not defile them, but what comes out of their mouth, that is what defiles them" (Matthew 15:11). And ever since then, some critics of Judaism—including some in the early church—have said that Judaism is more focused on external behavior than meaning. Even prominent liberal rabbis have derided the dietary laws as "kitchen Judaism," saying a focus on what foods to eat distracts us from appreciating the beliefs and values that matter most. But I think the dietary laws evocatively symbolize the belief that when it comes to living our faith, the little things are the big things. In other words, as my friend Michael Hyatt has put it, how we are in one thing tends to reflect how we are in everything.

A favorite story illustrates this idea. It comes from a famous British architect named Norman Foster. He was the lead architect for several of the residential dormitories at Cambridge University. He insisted on control over the design not only of the buildings, but of every permanent item within the buildings, including the plates and silverware. When he was asked why he required control over the cutlery, he replied by quoting another famous architect, Ludwig Mies van der Rohe, "God is in the details." The dietary laws remind us that God is in the details of the foods we eat, the times we eat them, and the ways we do so.

One aspect of the way we eat is the recitation of blessings. In Judaism, the term *blessing* is a technical term: it designates a specific class of prayers, those that begin with the words "Blessed are you, Eternal God, Sovereign of the universe."

The Hebrew word for blessed is *baruch*, and it comes from the Hebrew word for knees. Scholars suggest one of the earliest ways we praised and expressed gratitude toward God was the bending of our knees. Thus, saying a verbal blessing is a way of bowing before God.

Jews say blessings throughout the day: when we wake up in the morning, when we use the washroom, when we meet a new person, when we lie down for sleep. The Talmud urges us to say at least one hundred blessings every day.[2] Blessings are one of the ways we turn our homes and our lives into miniature sanctuaries.

Blessings thank God for providing for our needs. For example, the blessing after eating a meal—known as the *Birkat HaMazon*—is a riff on Deuteronomy 8:10, which says "When you have eaten your fill, give thanks to the Lord your God for the good land which He has given you" (author's translation). Notice the language of this commandment. We do not give thanks directly for the food. We give thanks to God for the land.

We depend on God for much more than physical sustenance. Our shelter, our livelihood, the air we breathe— all of them come from the land God has given us. The after-meal blessing is much longer than the before-meal blessing. Why? By saying an array of blessings after the meal, we are speaking to ourselves and to God at a critical moment. When we are hungry and about to eat, it feels natural to thank God. But when we are nourished, we may be tempted to think we don't need God. Complacency breeds arrogance. We prepared our meal. We harvested the land. We set the table. *God*, we might think to ourselves, *had nothing to do with it*. It is precisely at that moment that we need to spend time saying blessings. Saying them brings us outside of ourselves. We remind ourselves of our dependence upon God and one another. Blessings sustain faith.

Another common blessing helps us see how this works: the blessing we say before drinking sacred wine. The wine is known as the *kiddish*. The word *kiddish*, as you might surmise, is made up of the same Hebrew letters as the word *kadosh*, which we learned means holiness. Before we drink the wine, we say a blessing to God who has "created the fruit of the vine." The blessing is not over the wine. The blessing is to God who creates the wine. The wine itself is not holy. Rather, the act of blessing God and consuming the wine brings us closer to God, the source of holiness.

This is different from the role of Communion in some Christian communities. In the Catholic Church and some other churches, the communion wine itself undergoes transformation, and becomes the blood of Christ. In Judaism the wine is still wine. But the blessing of God and consumption of the wine puts us in a state of greater holiness. We say this anytime we drink a juice or wine. We say an extended version of the blessing on Shabbat. The extended blessing emphasizes that God sanctifies the wine in the same way God sanctified the seventh day of the week. God sets the wine apart to bring us into a state of holiness in the way God set apart the seventh day as a way to bring us rest.

Separation makes holiness. When we say a blessing, we set apart the experience we are about to undergo. We make it sacred. We are modeling ourselves on God. Blessings bridge heaven and earth. The Jewish sages used this idea to help resolve a seeming contradiction in the Bible. Psalm

24 says, "The earth is the LORD's and the fullness thereof" (Psalm 24:1 ESV). But then later in the Psalms we read, "The heavens are God's heavens, but the earth He gave to humans" (Psalm 115:16, author's translation). How do the rabbis make sense of the seeming contradiction? Does the earth belong to God or to human beings? The Talmud says, "The first position is true if humans take of the earth without offering a blessing. But the latter is true if gratitude is expressed through a blessing."[3] Blessings are an acknowledgment of God's gifts to us. They are our way of accepting God's gift with gratitude.

BLESSING THE MOMENTS

Not just material goods like food and wine can be sanctified by a blessing. Life experiences can also occasion blessings and become sources of holiness. An experience my first year in the rabbinate drove this home to me. I was at the temple when a man rushed into my study. "Could you chat for a minute?" he asked. We sat down and he asked me if I knew the words of a blessing he had just heard. He didn't know how it went except that it started "Baruch Atah Adonai."

"OK," I said, "it could be anything. Can you tell me where you heard it?"

"Yes. I was in New York last week and having dinner at a restaurant. Just a few tables away from me, right as I was eating, a man proposed to his girlfriend. She said yes, and everybody in the restaurant cheered. Then the man walked quietly over to a corner, put on a yarmulke [the traditional

Jewish head covering, which some men wear all the time and some don specifically for prayer], and said some type of blessing. Both their eyes filled with tears. I barely heard what he said but it was quite short."

"The blessing," I said, "may have been the shechyanu. Did it go like this: Baruch atah, Adonai Eloheinu, Melech haolam, shehecheyanu, v'kiy'manu, v'higiyanu laz'man hazeh?"

He said "That's it!" and then he asked if I had a copy.

"Yes, absolutely," I said.

"Good. I am planning to propose to my girlfriend this weekend, and I want to say it with her."

That blessing that young man was so interested in is known as the shechyanu. We say it at moments we deem sacred and special. Those moments are often firsts—like the first time our child ties his shoe or the first day of a new job or the first day in a given summer that we eat a piece of sweet watermelon. We also often say the shechyanu at major life milestones like weddings or anniversaries. And, apparently, at proposals!

The couple in the New York restaurant was speaking not just to God, but to total strangers: their blessing of gratitude became a source of inspiration to someone they'd never even met.

UNTRADITIONAL BLESSINGS

Even though blessings follow a certain linguistic formula, they express our feelings. They are words that come simultaneously from our prayer books and from the heart.

And as one of the great Jewish sages taught, "Words from the heart enter the heart."

One of the ways I often think of blessings in Judaism is as the language of sacred relationship. The primary relationship is the one we have with God. Blessings are a way we sustain that relationship. In the same way two spouses or friends will have a shared language—familiar names they call each other or words that echo shared experiences—so we have a language shared with God. Blessings are the core of that relationship.

Blessings work because of the power of words. In Judaism words are not simply sounds coming out of our mouth. Words lift up. Words tear down. Words destroy. Words create. Indeed, the Torah shows us that God creates the world through words. God says, "Let there be light," and then there is light. The Hebrew word for "word" is *devar*. *Devar* also means "thing." Words are not just symbols. They have weight to them, even if we cannot see that heft.

This view seems countercultural today. Perhaps you are familiar with the nursery rhyme "Sticks and stones may break my bones but words will never hurt me." The point of the rhyme is to get children to settle disputes with words rather than physical violence. But the conclusion is false. Words do hurt us. And they help us. They transform relationships. We have the opportunity to bless others through our words, even words that do not begin "Baruch Atah Adonai . . ."

I experienced this near the end of my grandfather's life. He passed away in 2007. Up until his death, I tried to talk to or visit him every day. We would usually end our conversations with my saying, "Talk to you tomorrow." I did not say to him, as I usually do to my parents or my wife,

"I love you." He was not a warm fuzzy kind of guy, and declaring love just did not feel right. But during those last few weeks, something changed. Perhaps it was the birth of my daughter Hannah, or perhaps it was my grandfather's declining condition. Our moments became more fused with meaning. A month before he died, I was sitting by his bed, and we were talking. As I got up to leave, I felt a twitch in my stomach. I turned to him and said, "Grandpa, I love you." He didn't say anything but the connection changed. Thereafter, we ended each conversation with my saying, "I love you."

And since then, I have understood that saying *I love you* to our dearest ones is a way of blessing them and blessing ourselves.

Blessings come from God and from us. Blessings connect us to God and to each other. The most powerful blessings do both at the same time. Perhaps that's why certain blessings have stood the test of time. Blessings like shechyanu or the words *I love you* bespeak and speak to our deepest selves. We feel the presence of God when our blessings connect us. That's what the great Jewish theologian Martin Buber meant when he said God is the electricity surging between two human beings who are in authentic, attentive relationship to each other (Buber called that kind of relationship an I-Thou relationship).

In other words, God dwells where we let God in. There is a biblical verse that suggests this truth: "Let them build me a sanctuary so that I may dwell among them" (Exodus 25:8, author's translation). The Torah does not say dwell *in* it. It says dwell *among* them. Blessings create sanctuaries wherever we are. They let us create a home for God.

~~~~~~~~~

9

Life-Cycle
Events

~~~~~~~~~

A few years ago, I was asked to conduct an unusual wedding. The bride was a friend of a friend. She called to tell me that she was engaged. They had a wedding date set for the following June. Would I be available? "Sure," I replied. "But, there's more," she said softly. "My mom is dying. She has pancreatic cancer. She insists we not change our plans for the big ceremony in June."

Could I come to her mother's hospital room soon and perform a wedding ceremony? That way, her mom would have a chance to see her get married.

"Of course," I said. We set a date. When the time came, I went over to Northwestern Hospital in Chicago. I wore my usual office-casual attire: a striped button down shirt, gray pants, loafers. When I got to the hospital room, I quickly realized I had made a significant fashion mishap. The bride stood outside the room in a white wedding gown. The groom beamed next to her in a tuxedo. At least twenty-five friends in suits, ties, and dresses crowded the hospital room. They stood around the mom's bed. A hospital worker had brought in an electric keyboard and began playing. Four men brought in a chuppah (a Jewish wedding canopy) covered in flowers. The bride and groom entered to music and song.

Overwhelmed with emotion, I had trouble beginning the ceremony. We succeeded, however, in getting through it. By the end, there was not a dry eye in the room. When the groom followed Jewish tradition and broke a glass with his foot at the end of the wedding, everyone in the room said mazel tov (congratulations). We knew life had just given us a rare moment of beauty amid tragedy. About three weeks later, the bride's mother passed away.

That wedding ceremony brought a moment of joy and extraordinary meaning to the bride's mother's life—and at their best, that is what life-cycle rituals do, even in less dramatic circumstances than a hospital wedding. In this chapter we explore the life-cycle rituals of Judaism: weddings, funerals, births, and other rites of passage. We begin with funerals because that is the area where I have the most experience, and where I believe Judaism has the most to teach the world.

FUNERALS AND MOURNING

Baruch Dayan HaEmet—"Blessed be the Judge of Truth." Those are the words a Jew is supposed to recite as soon as he learns of a death. The Judge, of course, is God, and the requirement to bless God in the face of death captures something elemental about Jewish mourning practices. Our mourning practices invite us to acknowledge the reality of death and, even as we grieve, to accept what has happened. Indeed, the entire choreography of Jewish mourning can be seen as a path that helps us to accept death, to grieve, and then to move back into life. That path is marked by a series of rituals focusing intensely on the psychological and social needs of the mourners. Many Christians who have attended a Jewish funeral service or visited a house of mourning have told me how meaningful and rich the rituals are. As a rabbi, I know my deepest moments have come walking with mourners as they bury and remember their loved ones. One of the Hebrew words for the mourning process is *levayah*, which means "accompaniment." Symbolically, mourners accompany the deceased on their way to the hereafter, and members of the mourners' community accompany the bereaved into and through grief. Those "accompanyings" begin at the moment of death with "Baruch Dayan HaEmet": our God is the God of truth, and death is part of the truth of life on earth.

I often find that many Jews do not know the custom of saying the words "Baruch Dayan HaEmet." Therefore, whenever I learn of the death of a member of my synagogue or their relative and visit the mourners' homes, I begin our meeting asking those assembled to hold hands and say the blessing with me. It's powerful because it acknowledges what we often try to avoid or deny. During this meeting, I ask family members to talk about the deceased. I first ask people where the deceased was born and what they did for a living. These aren't particularly profound questions, but they get people talking. And once family members are talking, they become able to explore the deeper topics of values and legacy. I ask what role Judaism played in their life and what pursuits brought them the greatest meaning and joy. I ask about memorable experiences they shared with their loved one. Answering that helps mourners move to deeper places in their love of the deceased. The final question I ask is how the deceased shaped the way his or her family members live their own lives. This question reflects the way Jews' understanding that memory is not just something you do in your mind; we remember through the way we live.

Indeed, one of the most powerful prayers we read on Yom Kippur, the Day of Atonement and the holiest day of the year, pictures the lives of the deceased as seeds that fall into the ground and sprout up into magnificent trees through the descendants they leave behind.

At the end of this meeting, we prepare and walk through the funeral service. Because a dead body that is not yet buried is considered to be in a state of limbo—not alive on earth, but not yet in its final resting place—Jewish funerals typically takes place quite soon after a death. (Orthodox Jews aim for twenty-four hours or less.) It is also a traditional practice to refuse to leave the body alone. A family member stays with the body, even at a funeral home, or the family can engage someone known as a *shomer* (guardian) to stay with the body of the deceased and recite psalms. This practice of staying with the body is a way of comforting the soul of the deceased.

Some Jews also engage in a process known as *tahara* (purification) in which the body of the deceased is washed and then clad in a white ritual garment (called a *kittel*) for burial. Frequently, Jewish communities create burial societies in which the members agree to perform *tahara* for other members of the community. Members of my congregation who belong to burial societies have told me doing so is among the most moving and powerful religious experiences they have. Caring for a person in death reminds them of the uniqueness of every individual and the preciousness of the life we have.

Very few Jews hold a viewing of the deceased body. The Talmud teaches that we should be able to see another person only if they can see us. In other words, we should not look at someone who does not have the ability to look at us. A person's corpse does not have the ability to see us; therefore, we should not see him or her. Furthermore, Jews, believing that a body's decomposition should be as natural as possible, do not practice embalming. Most Jews do not practice cremation either, though more and more are doing so both for economic and environmental reasons.

After *tahara*, family members participate in a funeral service and burial. As we noted earlier, the sooner the service the better. But sometimes people's schedules require waiting a few days. In these circumstances, I often counsel families to wait and allow all those who wish to attend the funeral service to come. This permission reflects the value of *shalom bayit*, "peace in the home." In Jewish law, *shalom bayit* outweighs many other values because the Jewish sages saw peace in the home as a prerequisite for peace in the world. Giving all family members and close friends the opportunity to mourn at a funeral service helps preserve that peace.

In biblical and rabbinic times, the funeral service would begin with a procession starting from the home of the deceased. Today there is sometimes a procession of the deceased family members and the clergy into the sanctuary where the service is taking place. If the service takes place at the graveside, there is usually not a processional. The casket is typically plain wood. This custom reflects the rabbinic teaching that all are equal in death. A funeral is not a time to show off a person's wealth or status by using a fancy casket. A wooden casket also degrades naturally into the earth, allowing the body to decompose into the soil.

The first ritual act is the mourners wearing and tearing a black ribbon. Tearing this black ribbon hearkens back to the biblical practice of rending one's clothing upon hearing of the death of a loved one. In the Bible, for example, Jacob rends his clothing when several of his sons tell him their brother Joseph is dead. This custom is known as *kriya*, which is the Hebrew word for tearing.

After *kriya*, we typically read a few psalms. Most prominent among them is Psalm 23, which contains the immortal words "The Lord is my Shepherd. I shall not want." Then the rabbi and/or family members will offer a *hesped*. *Hesped* is a Hebrew word often translated as "eulogy," but that translation misses some of the nuances of the Hebrew word. The purpose of a hesped is *nihum avelim*, which means "comforting the mourners." In other words, the purpose of a hesped is not only to describe and praise the deceased. It is just as important to comfort those who are mourning. Usually little is said about the afterlife in a hesped. Rather, the hesped is about honoring the relationships among the deceased, the family, and the community in a comforting way.

I've been in situations where the deceased was a serious criminal or someone about whom it was difficult to say many positive or comforting words. In those cases, Jewish tradition is to curtail the service and simply say very little about the deceased, though if *something* positive can be said, it should be. In this vein, I once conducted a service for a man who was active in the Chicago mafia. His son delivered the hesped. He began by acknowledging that his father did a lot of illegal things. "But," he continued, "he was a wonderful grandfather."

The hesped is followed by a prayer called *El molei rachamim*, which means "God, full of mercy." This prayer does acknowledge the afterlife, pleading with God for the soul of the deceased to be "bound up in the bond of everlasting life." This phrase comes from the Book of Isaiah, and is often abbreviated by the acronym T'N'. You can find the acronym on many Jewish headstones. I think of it as the Hebrew equivalent of "May he rest in peace." Unlike the kaddish, the *El molei rachamim* prayer is often chanted. Traditionally, it was the only music considered appropriate in a Jewish funeral service. Today, however, many synagogues will include favorite hymns or songs in the service.

If the service is held in a sanctuary or a hall, the *El molei rachamim* is the last prayer of the service. Immediately after it is finished, the mourners will accompany the family and the casket out of the sanctuary. Pallbearers selected by the family typically carry the casket, and the rest of the family and mourners follow silently. I think of this silent filing out of the sanctuary as a symbol of the respect of the mourners for the deceased. The silence also marks it as an unusual occurrence, a time when we step out of our world as it normally is. Scholars call these moments liminal times. A funeral is a liminal time where our normal day-to-day life is interrupted so that we can ponder memory and eternity.

The funeral service then moves to the cemetery. The cemetery service is shorter than the sanctuary service and typically contains three main rituals. The first is a committal prayer, usually said as or before the body is lowered into the grave. The second is the covering of the casket and filling of the grave. The way a grave is filled in a Jewish funeral service differs from what I have experienced in secular or other religious settings. At a Jewish burial service, almost all the mourners participate in the burial by placing earth into the grave. (Some people say placing "dirt" into the grave, but

I learned at my first funeral service that some people find the word *dirt* disrespectful! Therefore, I always say "earth.") We participate because of the importance of accompanying the deceased to the grave. We are accompanying the deceased as closely as we can. I also tell the mourners who participate that they are doing a good deed for the deceased that can never be repaid. Often in life, we do things because we get something out of it. We work in order to get paid and provide for our family, for example. But when we shovel earth into the grave of a loved one, it's an act of love and respect that has no recompense.

In performing this act, you can either directly lift the earth and place it into the grave or use a shovel to do so. Typically you take three handfuls or shovelfuls of earth. Doing it three times signifies true intent to honor the deceased. Sometimes participants fill the entire grave. Other times each person does three handfuls or shovelfuls and a machine does the rest. Following the burial, the kaddish (the primary Jewish prayer of mourning) is recited, and mourners form a path for the family members to walk back to the hearse.

In October 2018, the day after a gunman walked into a synagogue in Pittsburgh and murdered eleven Jews at prayer, the *Pittsburgh Post-Gazette* published a front-page headline in Hebrew: the opening words of the mourner's kaddish. It was the first time I am aware of when a Hebrew prayer was featured on the front page of a major American newspaper. I felt a mixture of pride and anger. I was proud that the words of an ancient Hebrew prayer could bring comfort and perspective to a nation shocked at these horrific murders. But I also felt extraordinary anger that a sacred place had become a place of bloodshed. I pictured what it would have looked like in my own sanctuary. And I felt a profound sadness at how many people would now be saying this prayer of mourning for the people who had been murdered. I imagine I might think of the Pittsburgh shooting during the kaddish of funerals in my own community for many years to come.

After the funeral comes the *shiva*; shiva is a Hebrew word for "seven," and in the context of mourning, it refers to the practice of marking the first seven days after the death of a close relative. During the shiva, mourning family members stay in their homes receiving visitors for the seven days following a funeral. Shiva begins when the family members of the deceased arrive at their home after the burial. The first thing they do is eat an egg. Explanations for this practice vary, but one compelling gloss is that an egg symbolizes life, and shiva is the beginning of the process of reintegrating into life after the shock of death.

During the period of shiva, friends and acquaintances visit the mourners at their home. These are not social visits. The purpose is to comfort the mourners and ensure they are not alone. I've witnessed the psychological wisdom of this practice many times. When we are mourning, we can turn inward. We can create ways for blaming ourselves for not doing enough to support or express love for the deceased. We can become mired in anger and frustration and melancholy. We can feel as if we want to be alone. But the presence of others helps us cope. We remind ourselves that life goes on even though the life of our loved one has ended. The presence of others lifts us out of ourselves.

Those who come to the house of mourners during shiva should not expect to be entertained. The custom is that they do not speak to the mourning family members unless the family members initiate the conversation. Mourners also cover the mirrors in their homes. Mirrors symbolize vanity. They reflect our concern with how we appear to the outside world. That should not be a concern during mourning. We are held by others. We do not need to impress or satisfy them.

Each evening of the shiva includes a prayer service. The prayer service gives the mourners an opportunity to say the kaddish, which Jewish law teaches can only be said when ten or more people are together in prayer. The familiarity of the prayers, sung in familiar, comfortable melodies, draws people out of their heads and into their hearts—and it draws people toward God.

During the shiva, mourning family members typically do not leave the house. Some people have said this practice feels too restrictive and that getting back into daily life would be more comforting because it would take them away from focusing on loss and sadness. That is exactly the way I used to feel, but experiences with my congregation have shown me the true depth of the traditional Jewish practice. We need to experience the sadness and mourning before we can enter fully back into daily life.

That's the lesson taught to me by Bernie, a member of my first congregation. His wife died in her early thirties. They had four children: two were in high school, one in middle school, and the other was five. They were heartbroken. The congregation supported the family with meals and rides and child care. But, as he told me later, Bernie pushed his oldest boys to go back to school the day after the funeral. He thought it would help them get their lives back to normal.

It seemed to work for a while. But several years later, when the boys were in college, they told him how angry they were that he sent them back to school. They never had the time or opportunity to mourn. They lost their mom, and the next day they had to prepare for a geometry quiz. The truth was, they could never return to normal. They had to grieve the past and adjust to a *new* normal in which their mother was no longer alive. Bernie told me he regretted pushing them back into school.

Still, the shiva does end, and mourners take several steps back toward ordinary routines. The shiva is followed by a thirty-day period known as *sheloshim*, when mourners typically go back to work or resume other regular responsibilities, but avoid large public gatherings and celebrations, and continue saying the kaddish. After the *sheloshim*, mourners take yet another step out of mourning-practice and into regular time, resuming attendance at large gatherings—yet the formal period of mourning lasts a year, during which some Jews mourning a parent, child, or sibling will say the kaddish every day. (I encourage mourners to say it at least weekly.)

No amount of ritual can drain away the sting of grief; what Jewish mourning ritual does, I think, is recognize that grief has different moments, different phases—and that grief is to be neither evaded nor fetishized, but held as part of life.

BRIS/BABY NAMING

Just as Judaism ritualizes death, so it also marks birth. A bris is the ceremony in which a male child is circumcised and given a Hebrew name. During a bris ceremony, the circumcision is performed in a ritualized manner by a trained officiate known as a *mohel*, and it is accompanied by prayers and songs. The first bris for a newborn occurred when Abraham circumcised his son Isaac.

A bris can feel uncomfortable the first time you witness one. And I confess a bris can feel uncomfortable even if you've witnessed dozens of them. The baby cries incessantly, and we wonder why we are performing this seemingly primitive ritual. The biblical reason given for ritual circumcision is that it is a physical, embodied marker of the sacred covenant between God and the family of Abraham. According to the Bible, those who are not circumcised are "cut off" from the Jewish people. It is one of the few biblical commandments that specifies an extremely harsh punishment for those who fail to observe it. Even secular Jews like Sigmund Freud considered circumcision so important that he advised indifferent Jewish parents to circumcise their sons because otherwise they would be robbing him of the chance to feel authentically Jewish as an adult. Circumcision, in other words, is a potent physical and psychological marker of Jewish identity.

Circumcision does not, however, serve the same function as baptism. To be sure, different Christian communities attach different meanings to baptism. But as a generalization, we can say that throughout much of church history, baptism marked formal entry into God's people. In Judaism, however, circumcision does not confer identity. Rather, it *marks* identity. A child is Jewish if his or her mother is Jewish, and a boy's not being circumcised does not mean he is not a part of the Jewish people. According to the Jewish sages' interpretation of Genesis, the consequence of a male Jew's not being circumcised is that he will *feel spiritually cut off* from Judaism; he is not in any sense excommunicated.

I find there is no comfortable way of explaining circumcision except to say that we do some things in life even though we do not completely understand why. Circumcision is an act of humility and respect in the face of a four-thousand-year-old tradition begun by our ancestor Abraham. No evidence exists that it harms infants, and research over the last several decades has also suggested circumcision may have some marginal health benefits. Experiencing the seeming mystery of circumcision with humility can make the ceremony all the more powerful. Parents and grandparents respond in unexpected and moving ways.

Last year, for example, I led the prayers at a bris at the home of a member of the congregation. (A doctor who is also trained as a *mohel* performed the circumcision, while I led the prayers. This is a typical arrangement.) The parents and grandparents at this particular bris tended to be serious people—formal, proper. We proceeded through the circumcision, and I invited friends and family to say their wishes or hopes for the baby. Well, the great-grandmother came up and presented a book to her great-grandson—the same book she had given copies of to her three sons and their six sons when they had their bris. As she explained why the book was significant, she began to cry, as did everyone else in the living room. It was that ritual of the bris over three generations that gave this grandmother the space to express her love, to honor a tradition, to tie the family together through the gift of this book and the values and history it represented—all of that came about because of this mysterious sacred ritual.

Over the last forty years, Jewish leaders have also developed rituals around the birth of baby girls. When our daughters were born, my wife and I had special naming ceremonies eight days after their births. We gave and celebrated their Hebrew names, and we prayed for their health of body and spirit. Parents will often choose Hebrew names for their children, and these names are used in ceremonial occasions like B'nei Mitzvah and weddings (see below). The custom of having a special Hebrew name goes back to the Book of Genesis, where God gives Abram the name Abraham, and Sarai the name Sarah. Like circumcision, names can symbolize the covenant between God and the Jewish people.

For many families, the idea of covenant means family and tradition, and they choose a Hebrew name as a way to remember a deceased grandparent or great-grandparent. They often either give a child her ancestor's exact name or choose a name that begins with the same letter the ancestor's name began with. For example, our daughter Hannah was named for her great-grandmother Harriett. She had died two years before Hannah's birth, and at the naming ceremony, we talked about Harriett's love of family, her integrity, her financial acumen, her simple joy in life—and our hopes for Hannah to embody those qualities in her own way. A Hebrew name links the generations.

BNEI MITZVAH

One of the ways Judaism marks our growth as human beings is a ceremony known as a Bar/Bat Mitzvah. A Bar

Mitzvah is the name of the ceremony for boys, and it is Bat Mitzvah for girls. (Bnei Mitzvah is the plural.) It is a ceremonial rite of passage where the boy or girl reads from the Torah scroll and leads the congregation in worship and becomes responsible for following the commandments. In ancient times, after becoming a Bar Mitzvah, the young man was expected to pray three times daily, as Jewish law prescribes; follow the dietary laws; fast on appropriate holidays; and observe the other commandments.

The Bar Mitzvah ritual is two thousand years old; the first Bat Mitzvah happened in 1922 in America, and it is now commonplace for non-Orthodox Jews.

Until recently, becoming a Bar Mitzvah did not involve an extended party and celebrations. Rather, immediate family came to the synagogue, and listened to the Bar Mitzvah boy say the Torah blessing; then his father recited a prayer absolving himself of responsibility for his son's behavior. The son was now responsible for his actions. That meant following the commandments—and in some cases, it also meant earning a living.

My grandfather was raised in an Orthodox Jewish family, and he had such a Bar Mitzvah in Milwaukee in 1925. Right after he became a Bar Mitzvah, the rabbi gave him a set of *tefillin*—Jewish leather bands we wrap around the arm and fingers during morning prayer—and expected him to don them daily. Not coincidentally, it was after he became a Bar Mitzvah that my grandfather got his first job. (It was also during the beginning of the Great Depression, so his family probably needed it!)

For him—as it has been for Jews throughout history— becoming a Bar Mitzvah honored the importance of the

Torah. In Judaism, the Torah is our evidence for God's presence on earth. It is our guide and truth. A Bar or Bat Mitzvah reading from the Torah gives visual evidence of our commitment to the vitality and message of Torah. When a Bar or Bat Mitzvah reads from the Torah surrounded by parents and grandparents, we see the evidence that Jewish commitment survives from generation to generation. The Hebrew phrase is *l'dor vah dor*. When I became a Bar Mitzvah, my grandfather held the Torah and passed it to my mom, who passed it to my dad, and my dad passed it to me. My mom then sang a hymn based on the words *l'dor vah dor*.

Today a Bar or Bat Mitzvah ceremony is less about assuming new formal responsibility than it is about recognizing a child's ongoing growth with a sacred ceremony. It is a way of marking time and making sense of the changes experienced by children, parents, families, and communities. I have noticed that a Bar or Bat Mitzvah celebration changes the parents as much as it changes the thirteen-year-old child. They recognize they have grown along with their children. They glimpse a future in which their child will become an adult. I suspect they feel their own mortality as well. They are no longer parents of young children. They have become parents of adolescents on their way to adulthood.

As my wife, Ari, who is also a rabbi, observed to me, the Bar or Bat Mitzvah ceremony also shapes the friends and extended family of the Bar or Bat Mitzvah. Ari's work centers around interfaith families who are raising their children with two religions. Most of these families choose to celebrate Bar and Bat Mitzvah because they see the power of this ritual to tie families together and mark a meaningful moment in life. They feel the vibrancy of faith and God's presence as a young person reads from the Torah, and they feel pride that they helped nurture this Bar or Bat Mitzvah to this moment in life. For interfaith families, the Bar or Bat Mitzvah can be a moment to recognize that that they have indeed found a way to do the difficult work of honoring the complexity of the family's religious life.

WEDDINGS

We began this chapter with a wedding I conducted in a hospital room. We'll end with my favorite wedding scene from a movie. No, it's not from the *Wedding Crashers* or *The Wedding Singer*. It's from *Fiddler on the Roof*. Here's the backstory: the bride and groom are in love, but they have struggled to get to this moment. Tevye, the bride's father, wanted his daughter to marry a rich man rather than the poor groom. He had promised her to someone else but then broke the engagement after she pleaded with him to do so. When the wedding with the man she loves finally takes place, the entire town, including the rejected earlier groom, is present at the ceremony. Old animosities and tensions are set aside for a moment as an entire community celebrates. It's not only touching but also instructive in that the presence of the entire community reminds us that marriages both support and are supported by the community. In Judaism, a wedding is not simply a ceremony marking the marriage of a bride and groom. If it was only that, the couple could simply come to the rabbi's office and sign the Jewish marriage license known as a *ketubah*. Rather, it is a communal expression of support. The entire town had a role in bringing the bride and groom together because the entire town shaped the culture of the community in which they became adults.

Like a Bar or Bat Mitzvah, a wedding ties together the past, present, and future. The marrying couple's parents are experiencing the ascent of a new generation. The babies they once held are creating their own household. They will bring the next generation into the world.

A Jewish wedding also embodies Judaism's tendency to express itself in *belonging* as well as *believing*. In *Fiddler on the Roof*, the spurned fiancé may not have wanted to attend the wedding. But he was part of the community. And the Talmud says, "Do not separate yourself from the community." Being at the wedding expresses his faith and belonging to the Jewish community more than his affection for the couple getting married.

The Jewish wedding ceremony tries to capture this sense of community in one of its ritual items, the chuppah—the canopy within which the bride and groom stand during the ceremony. The chuppah consists of four poles and a cover on top. It can be freestanding or stationary. The critical requirement is that the four sides are open and unimpeded. This openness conveys the hope that the bride and groom's home is open and welcoming to the wider community. They welcome others into their lives. At the same time, only the bride and groom stand directly within the chuppah. Their relationship is unique. Unlike other family relationships, which are usually biological, they have chosen to spend life with each other. The chuppah—like the entire wedding ceremony—both sets the couple apart and underlines their ongoing connection to the larger community.

Perhaps the most famous Jewish wedding ritual is the breaking of the glass. This happens at the end of the ceremony. Before the kiss, the groom will shatter a wine glass (or a light bulb, which is especially easy to break), with his foot. Scholars do not know where or why this custom began. It might have begun because of a superstition that loud sounds ward off evil spirits from the happy couple. Over time many Jews began to connect the breaking of the glass with the destruction of the temple by the Romans in 70 CE. That event embodies all the tragic experiences of Jewish history. Thus, even at a time of joy like a wedding, we break a glass to remember that life is not always easy. We will experience tragedy and loss.

I have conducted more than five hundred wedding ceremonies, and they have been the most joyous parts of my ministry. Part of the reason they feel so important is that marriage is so hard. We need the celebration and support of others to help guide us—and both celebration and support begin at the wedding.

Life-cycle rituals offer us a framework with which to make sense of the experiences of life. They name aspirations and hold memories, and they bind us to our community and to God.

10

The Eternal Questions

There is a story told by the Nobel Prize–winning physicist Isidor Rabi. When he was a boy and would come home from school each day, his mother would not ask what he learned or how he'd done on his tests. She would say, "Izzy, did you ask a good question today?"[1] Questions lead us to knowledge. And knowledge deepens commitment. Rather than represent doubt, questions in Judaism symbolize a search for truth. Many of the great discussions in the Talmud begin with questions. One of the best-selling Jewish books of all time is titled *The Jewish Book of Why*. Thus, consistent with Jewish tradition, we will end this book by asking and answering a series of questions. I also invite you to ask me questions by e-mailing me at emoffic@gmail.com.

What Do Jews Believe About Jesus?

I am asked this question almost weekly, and I wrote an entire book about it. The short answer is that many Jews know little about Jesus one way or the other, but they tend to think of him as a historical figure who began one of the great world religions. Many also know that he was a learned rabbi and teacher. But Jews do not believe that Jesus was God or the messiah. Because of the long history of anti-Semitism in Christianity, some Jews express an aversion to the word *Jesus*. They associate his name with persecution of Jews.

Much of my writing and speaking as a rabbi is dedicated to changing this perception and seeing Jesus as a bridge for conversation and engagement rather than a barrier to real learning.

Here are three ways modern Jews might think about Jesus. I offer them not because I necessarily agree with all of them, but when people of faith respect one another's differences and convictions, we build a world more welcoming of the one God.

1. Jesus Was a Jewish National Hero: Orthodox Rabbi Shmuley Boteach emphasizes Jesus's self-understanding and significance as a political leader of first-century Jews:

> The more we peel away the surface, the more we see the truth: Jesus, I will continue to show, was a great political leader who fought for the liberation of his people. In this sense, he saw himself in the guise of Moses and David, both of whom, while supremely concerned with the spiritual welfare of the people, were first and last concerned with the political freedom of the Jewish nation.[2]

In other words, for Jews of the time, Jesus was a political hero and not a spiritual one.

2. Jesus Was a Rabbi: The great nineteenth- and early twentieth-century American Rabbi Emil Hirsch wrote and spoke frequently about Jesus. He saw him as a champion of faith in human progress and a teacher of the Old Testament. As Hirsch proclaimed from the pulpit, "He was of us; he is of us. We quote the rabbis of the Talmud; shall we then, not also quote the rabbi of Bethlehem? Shall not he in whom

there burned, if it burned in any one, the spirit and the light of Judaism, be reclaimed by the synagogue?"[3] Hirsch's point of view has been echoed in several contemporary books with the phrase "Rabbi Jesus" in their title.

3. Jesus Was an Ethical Exemplar: Emil Hirsch's brother-in-law Kaufmann Kohler was also a prominent rabbi and scholar. He was president of the seminary for Reform rabbis for twenty-five years. He wrote frequently about Jesus, and while he was critical of Jesus's seeming dismissal of the law of the Old Testament, he highlighted his social message. For Kohler, Jesus was a "helper of the poor" and a "sympathizing friend of the fallen."[4] He said Jesus learned these values at the synagogue and brought them to the forefront of first-century Jewish life.

WHAT, IF ANYTHING, DOES JUDAISM TEACH ABOUT HEAVEN AND HELL?

Another way to phrase this question is to ask what Judaism teaches about the afterlife. And the answer is: it's complicated. Most sacred Jewish texts affirm some part of us survives after our physical life has ended. These texts do not, however, offer much specificity on what that afterlife looks like.

Some texts—including major sections of the Talmud—suggest that our souls survive when our physical life has ended. But at the "end of days"—the time when the messiah arrives on earth and transforms history—our souls and bodies will reunite and we will come to life again. This resurrection will begin in the holy of city of Jerusalem.

This belief has led many Jews to choose to be buried on the Mount of Olives, which is as close to the city of Jerusalem as it is possible to be buried.

Other texts do not go into as much detail about the connection between soul and body. They do, however, describe what the experience will be in the afterlife. Their vision reflects the values they hold. That is, they imagine an afterlife that reinforces the values they hold on earth. We see this truth in two passages from Jewish texts.

The first passage is found in the Talmud. The passage is ostensibly about rabbinic views of a skin disease, but it is really about rabbinic authority, and, even more subtly, it is about the afterlife. The most interesting part of the passage is its first sentence: "They were arguing in the academy of heaven." We do not usually associate heaven with arguing. Yet, here is a group *arguing* while in heaven. And what does heaven look like? It is not filled with clouds and angels strumming on harps. Rather, it is an "academy." In other words, for this group of Jewish sages, heaven is a giant school. Their idea of paradise is sitting and arguing in a study hall.

What makes this study hall special, however, is that God is the teacher. And God is even participating in the discussion. The rabbis and God are arguing about a minute detail of Jewish law. One of the arguments ends with the final decision being made not by God, but by one of the rabbis!

I once taught this text to a group at a church where I was speaking. It elicited much surprise, even frustration. How can God be wrong and a human being be right? If God decides something, isn't that the right decision by definition? Not in the rabbinic worldview. The rabbis saw the world as governed by a divinely ordained system of law. God established the system, but within that system, human beings have the authority to make decisions. God is like a parent who helps guide their children to learn how to make decisions. Arriving at the right decisions requires learning and discussion. That learning is the essence of life, and even God cherishes the process. Thus, according to the rabbis, heaven is an endless series of study and discussion.

The other notable picture of the afterlife is found not in the Talmud, but in the writings of leaders of the Hasidic movement. The Hasidic movement arose in eighteenth-century Europe, and its leaders rebelled against the austerity and intellectual focus of most rabbinic leaders and instead focused on spirituality, simplicity, and joy. They resembled Christian movements like the Quakers and Shakers in their approach. Among the Hasids, what was most important about a person was not knowledge or ritual observance, but kindness and character.

We see this approach in a story told about one rabbi. According to his followers, this rabbi had the power to travel to heaven and to hell. After returning from heaven and hell, the rabbi told his people about them. He described hell as a place with people surrounding a table with a sumptuous meal. Yet, they were emaciated. They wailed and screamed as they tried to grasp the food. What stopped them from getting the food? Their arms. Each person had a spoon, but their arms were splinted with wooden slats, so they could not bend either elbow to bring the food to their mouths.

The rabbi then arrived in heaven. At first, he was shocked. It looked the same. A group of people surrounded a sumptuous meal. They also held spoons. They also had their arms splinted with wooden slats. But instead of wailing and crying, they were smiling and laughing. What they figured out was that they could not pull their spoons to their own mouths. But they could use the spoons to feed one another. And that is what they did. One person would lower his spoon, fill it with food, and the feed the person across from him. They fed one another. That made it heaven. The difference between heaven and hell is shaped by the way we act here on earth. Giving, kindness, sacrifice is the way we get to heaven.

Do Jews Believe in a Messiah?

As noted above, traditional Judaism does not believe Jesus was the messiah or God. Yet, Jewish texts do envision the coming of a messiah. That messiah will usher in an era of peace and harmony and restoration of the Jewish state and monarchy with a new ruler descended from King David. This vision is found in early Jewish texts, though its importance is downplayed in later texts as Jewish teachings became more focused on worldly practices rather than messianic visions.

The word *messiah* itself did not originally refer to a divine figure who would transform the world. Rather, the Hebrew word *meh-she-ach* means "anointed one." A messiah was someone anointed with oil. This anointing took place before a monarch ascended to the throne.

The most prominent and celebrated monarch was David. David brought the twelve Israelite tribes together to form one United Kingdom. He achieved great victories and was beloved by God. He is credited with writing many of the psalms found in the Bible. But after the reign of David's son Solomon, the kingdom split into two nations—Judah and Israel. Those nations bickered and both were eventually destroyed. The era of David's sovereignty was seen by later generations as a golden age. When picturing the ideal future, Jews thought of the era of David and imagined one of his descendants on the throne. Thus, the word *messiah* evolved to mean not only someone anointed for kingship but also a human being anointed to usher in divine redemption.

Until the nineteenth century, most Jews believed that such a messiah would eventually arrive on earth. They prayed for it daily. Indeed, the first followers of Jesus were all Jews who believed he was the Messiah. But in subsequent eras, several false messiahs arose and generated the loyalty of hundreds of thousands of people. One of these false messiahs named Sabbatai Tzvi captivated millions of Jews in Eastern Europe in the seventeenth century until his popularity attracted the attention of a Turkish sultan, and Tzvi was thrown into prison and soon converted to Islam. The sense of betrayal felt by many of his followers—along with the changes in intellectual and political life in the eighteenth century—led many rabbis to rethink the concept of the messiah. Instead of focusing on identifying the messiah as an individual who would bring about redemption, they focused on the eventual arrival of a messianic era in which people and nations would live in peace and harmony. A statement from a group of rabbis in 1885 captured this philosophy succinctly: "We recognize, in the modern era of universal culture of heart and intellect, the approaching of the realization of Israel's great Messianic hope for the establishment of the kingdom of truth, justice, and peace among all men."[5]

Some Jews did remain committed to the vision of an individual messiah, but today most remain attached to the vision of a messianic era. And there's a strong sense in Jewish texts that messianic expectation should not be the sole focus of one's imagination. One Talmudic teaching makes the point: if you are planting a tree and the messiah arrives, you are supposed to finish planting the tree and only then stand up, walk over, and greet him.[6] In other words, we need to stay grounded in the work of this earth, and not escape the here and now by focusing on awaited redemption.

IS HUMAN NATURE GOOD OR EVIL?

The Torah seems to offer conflicting views on this question. In the first chapter of Genesis, we read that human beings are "created in God's image" (1:27). That seems to suggest an inherent goodness. But then in Genesis 8—shortly before God sends the flood to destroy the earth except for Noah and his family—God says, "the devisings of man are evil from his youth" (v. 21, author's translation). The two approaches conflict with one another.

One resolution to this dilemma is the Christian idea of original sin. Human beings started off good. But Adam and Eve ate from the tree God prohibited. Their defiance tainted humankind.

Jewish theology does not include a concept of original sin. I like to say that Judaism teaches an "original split." In other words, our natural inclinations are split. Part of everyone—a part that in Judaism is known as the *yetzer harah*, the evil inclination—inclines toward sin. The yetzer harah (somewhat similar to what Sigmund Freud called the id) generates aggression, envy, violence. The other part of us, the *yetzer tov*, inclines toward the good. It manifests itself in kindness, charity, and morality. Every person has both inclinations.

We might think that we should strive to live by the *yetzer hatov* and eliminate the yetzer harah. But the rabbis saw this approach as too simplistic. Instead of eliminating the yetzer harah, the goal of faith and Jewish practices is to channel it. It is to take the energy of the yetzer harah and use it to improve the world. The Talmud teaches that without the yetzer harah, we would not build cities or have children. In other words, evil inclinations can nonetheless lead somewhere good. Maimonides said that, over time, those who live a life of faith express the good inclination more and more. It is thus—choosing life; increasing day by day the ways we give expression to the yetzer tov—that we mend the original split.

WHAT ARE THE DIFFERENCES AMONG THE JEWISH DENOMINATIONS? WHAT ARE REFORM, CONSERVATIVE, AND ORTHODOX JUDAISM?

This question is among the first I get whenever I speak about Judaism at churches. Like most other religious groups, Jews have lots of internal differences of opinion.

The key theological difference is the way the denominations understand the Torah. Orthodox Jews believe the Torah is the Word of God revealed directly to Moses atop Mount Sinai. A key phrase used to describe this theological view is "Torah from Heaven." Torah demands absolute fidelity because it is the Word of God. We may reinterpret parts of it, but we cannot reject or alter any of it because God gave it as it is.

This approach generally excludes critical scholarly study of the Torah because such study involves looking at the Torah in the context of the era in which it was written. But for most Orthodox Jews Torah is not the product of one or more human eras. It is God's eternal Word. Since Torah is God's eternal Word, the practices by which we follow Torah do not change substantially from generation to generation. Thus, Orthodox Jews understand themselves as following the same practices and way of life as their ancestors did over the last several thousand years. They follow the same *halakhah*—the Hebrew word means "the way" or "the path"—which is a set of laws found in and derived from the Torah. The Torah itself contains 613 laws, and the Talmud and commentaries on it contain thousands more. While not all Orthodox Jews follow all these laws, the guiding belief is that every Jew is bound by them.

Reform Judaism says that Torah is not the Word of God, but that it is a divinely inspired book written by human beings. We might say it is the voice of God filtered through human beings. Since Torah was written by human beings, Torah can be adapted by human beings. That does not mean we can change the words of Torah however and wherever we want, but we can see parts of it as reflecting the time in which it was written.

Reform Judaism also distinguishes between ritual and ethical laws. The ritual laws (such as rules about what we are forbidden to eat or what days we have to say certain prayers) are less important in Reform Judaism than the ethical laws (such as the Ten Commandments and the Golden Rule). This difference is not absolute, and sometimes ethical and ritual laws reinforce one another. But as a group of Reform rabbis put it in 1885,

> Today we accept as binding only its moral laws, and maintain only such ceremonies as elevate and sanctify our lives. . . . We hold that all such Mosaic and rabbinical laws as regulate diet, priestly purity, and dress originated in ages and under the influence of ideas entirely foreign to our present mental and spiritual state. They fail to impress the modern Jew with a spirit of priestly holiness.[7]

Today, Reform Jews have returned to some of the traditional rituals it rejected in the late nineteenth and early twentieth centuries. These include praying in Hebrew and following the dietary laws like not eating certain meats or mixing milk and meat. Yet, Reform Judaism remains focused more on the ethical than the ritual and does not hold either in principle or in practice that all Jews should follow the 613 commandments of the Torah or the others outlined in the Talmud.

Reform Judaism also embraces the critical study of the Torah. I teach a Bible study class every Saturday morning.

I like to use different commentaries, and among those I use are one from an Orthodox rabbi and another from a Reform rabbi. Certain issues are off-limits in the Orthodox commentary. It will not point out, for example, that Abraham could not have used camels because camels were not domesticated as animals until the tenth century BCE, and the chronology of the Bible suggests Abraham lived around 2000 BCE. The Reform commentary, however, would cite archaeologists and geologists on the domestication of camels and suggest that Abraham may have lived later than the Bible portrays. The Orthodox commentary might not point out that the long lives associated with some of the early biblical figures—Adam is said to have lived to nine hundred years and Abraham into his six hundreds—might be more mythological than real. The Reform commentary points out these numbers suggest the mythological role of these figures, and are not meant to be taken literally.

Conservative Judaism stands between Reform and Orthodoxy, but it generally falls closer to the Reform approach on matters of theology and to the Orthodox on matters of practice. Like Reform Judaism, Conservative Judaism sees the Torah as the divinely inspired word of human beings. Its rabbis and scholars embrace critical biblical scholarship and the discoveries of archaeology. Like Reform, Conservative Judaism permits women to become rabbis. An old joke says that the Conservative movement waits fifteen years and then does exactly what the Reform movement does.

On the level of practice, however, Conservative synagogues more closely resemble Orthodox ones. The worship service is almost all in Hebrew. Many of the prayers eliminated from a Reform service because of time or theology are included in a Conservative service. (On the other hand, women and men sit together in Conservative synagogues; Orthodox synagogues are sex-segregated. And, in Conservative synagogues, all leadership roles are open to women.) The rabbis and members of the synagogue are expected to follow the Jewish dietary laws and observe a traditional sabbath.

Conservative Judaism has often been seen as the middle ground in Jewish life. But just as the middle and the moderates have lost ground in politics today, so too the Conservative movement has lost ground in American Jewish life. For the first forty years after the Second World War, the Conservative movement was the largest denomination in American Jewish life. It has since shrunk significantly, and now the Reform movement is the largest without about 1.2 million members and nine hundred synagogues. One reason the Reform movement has grown into the largest is that its synagogues accept interfaith families as members and participants. Since 2005, about 80 percent of weddings of non-Orthodox Jews were interfaith weddings. The Reform movement currently counts 35 percent of American Jews as adherents. The Conservative movement is at 18 percent, and Orthodoxy is at 10 percent. About 36 percent of American Jews are not connected to any denomination.[8]

IS JUDAISM LEGALISTIC?

An old stereotype held that Jews care more about following the precise details of the law—of doing things right—than doing the right thing. They care more about the letter rather than the spirit of the law. The Old Testament, according to this view, depicts a God of vengeance and law, and the New Testament presents a God of love and forgiveness. Christianity, so this story goes, set aside this legalism as it developed into its own religion. Even as many Christians have set aside this stereotype, it still creeps up in sermons and even in secular publications.

The truth is that Judaism does embrace the role of law in religious life. The Torah contains 613 commandments, and Jews of all denominations seek to follow at least some of them. But a love of law does not come at the expense of the importance of love. Law and love are not contradictory. Rather, they reinforce each other. Think about a marriage. It is rooted in love. Yet, it also involves laws. These usually include monogamy, financial honesty, and parenting responsibilities. These laws are not usually enforced by an external body like the government. Rather, they exist as guidelines between the spouses themselves. The same is true in religion. God loves us, and we love God. As a result, we follow certain laws. We pray, we give, we serve others. We look to those who came before us for guidance. Jewish law does not have coercive power. Very few Jews have been excommunicated in history. Rather, following laws is an expression of love in religion, as it is in marriage. Forgiveness allows us to maintain our faith and our relationships when we make mistakes or disobey. Forgiveness is not the antithesis of law. It is its complement.

One Jewish legend says that God infused the world with two core forces: law and mercy. If God had only given us law, we would become a society of grudges and endless cycles of violence. We would have no way to repair relationships because we all make mistakes. So God gave us mercy. But if God had only given us mercy, we would have chaos. Laws give us order, predictability, and stability. Therefore, God gave us both. And they both shape the choices we make.

WHAT IS THE MOST IMPORTANT JEWISH HOLIDAY?

In most synagogues, there is a group called "twice-a-year Jews." These are members of the synagogue who attend worship on only two holidays: Rosh Hashanah—the Jewish New Year—and Yom Kippur, the day of atonement. When I was talking with a pastor friend about this phenomenon, he introduced me to the phrase "Chreasters." These are Christians who attend church only on Christmas and Easter. Sometimes Jews and Christians are more alike than we know!

Judging from the attendance spike, we might assume either Rosh Hashanah or Yom Kippur is the most significant Jewish holiday. And Yom Kippur is described in the Torah as the "Sabbath of Sabbaths." We fast and focus on prayer and self-reflection the entire day. Still, it is not the most important Jewish holiday.

The most important holiday is the weekly sabbath. Its uniqueness lies in its regularity. We celebrate the sabbath every week. We are reminded of beauty and purpose of God's creation every week. We are reminded of our commitment to learning, prayer, and acts of kindness every week. Seeing that regularity as a value requires a mind shift. We often associate value with scarcity. For example, pink star diamonds are valuable because they are rare. But the opposite is true in Judaism: the value of the sabbath lies in its regularity.

Regularity gives the Sabbath enormous influence. I came to understand this when I read the book *The Power of Habit* by Charles Duhigg. He shows the way our habits—what we do regularly and consistently—exert the greatest influence on our lives.[9] We are our habits. And when we observe Shabbat regularly, we experience a certain calm and peace and perspective. Those who have observed the sabbath regularly for decades seem to have a healthier perspective on life—they do not mistake the important for the urgent. They control time rather than letting time control them. I liken the impact of sabbath on our lives to the way ocean tides shape a rock on a beach. If you look at the rock every day, you would not notice any changes. But cumulatively, over the decades of constant water washing over the rock, you would see the rock transformed. Its edges would be smoother. Its surface would be more consistent. The sabbath transforms us in the same way. It does what faith does best: change our lives.

One other part of the sabbath makes it uniquely powerful. We can start small. I didn't always understand this. Early in my ministry, when people would ask me how they could start observing the sabbath, I would tell them to come to synagogue, make a sabbath dinner, come to Torah study, and devote most of the day to prayer and study. I don't think many people took me up on it. Now I simply say, "Light two candles at sundown on Friday. Say a blessing as you light them. Anything else you can do is a bonus."

WHY SHOULD CHRISTIANS LEARN ABOUT JUDAISM?

If you are Christian and have read this book, you've learned much about Judaism. Unless you are planning to convert, why would you learn about a faith you do not practice? We all have so much to learn about our own faiths. Why we spend time and effort learning about another?

Teaching and speaking in hundreds of churches has shown me that learning about the faith and practices of Jesus deepens the closeness many Christians feel toward Jesus. Jesus lived and died as a Jew. He taught the Hebrew Bible. He observed the Jewish holidays. He even celebrated a Bar Mitzvah. Pastor Brad Young eloquently captured what Christians can get from learning about Judaism when he wrote, "Our greatest challenge is to hear his authentic voice. Early Judaism provides the firm foundation for a proper understanding of Jesus and his Jewish theology."[10] Learning about Judaism changes the way Christians read the Bible and the meanings they see in prayers. It helps us understand more about what the Torah meant to Jesus as well as other followers of Jesus.

There is another deeply personal contemporary reason I believe Christians should learn about Judaism. For two thousand years Jews suffered enormous anti-Semitism. The Inquisition began in Christian Europe. So did the Holocaust. But over the last fifty years, relationships between Jews and Christians have improved dramatically. Interfaith families have grown. Priests and rabbis have gathered together for dialogue. Some churches and synagogues even share sacred space. When I have spoken and taught at churches, I have seen lives transformed by the knowledge of shared origins. I've seen Jews and Christians grow closer to God and to one another. When Christians seek to understand Judaism on its own terms, and when Jews seek to teach Torah in the open, loving way in which God gave it, we transcend our self-limiting boundaries and enrich our communities and ourselves.

The twentieth-century Hasidic leader Menachem Schneerson, known as the Rebbe, used to tell this apposite story: Three hundred years ago a rabbi needed to transport some precious rubies. There was no FedEx or UPS. He needed to find a trusted person to transport the precious stones.

So he interviewed two men. The first lived in his town. He had spent years hauling sacks of rocks. He was experienced. He was strong. He said he could do the job.

The second man had spent his years transporting diamonds. He was not in the same town as the owner of the rubies. He was not as strong as the first man. But he had spent his life transporting diamonds from town to town.

So whom did the rabbi pick? Did he pick the first man he knew? No. That man had spent his life only carrying rocks. He thought of stones simply as a burden to endure. They have weight but not worth. Rubies are more than he can comprehend.

The second man, however, may not have ever transported rubies. He may not know the rabbi. But he had carried diamonds. He knew what it meant to carry precious stones.

So it is, the Rebbe said, with our faith. When our faith is precious to us, we can appreciate how precious it is to others. We may see our faith as a diamond, and another person may see their faith as a ruby, but we know both are precious. By seeing how precious the diamonds of Torah and tradition are to the Jewish people, perhaps each of us can find more color and luster in the precious jewels we each carry in our hands and our hearts.

Notes

Introduction

1. Paula Frederickson, "When Jesus Celebrated Passover," *The Wall Street Journal*, April 19, 2019, www.wsj.com/articles /when-jesus-celebrated-passover-11555685683?mod=search results&page=1&pos=2.

1. God

1. Samuel Karff, *Permission to Believe* (Nashville: Abingdon Press, 2005), 52.

2. Karff, *Permission to Believe*, viii.

3. Francis Collins, *The Language of God: A Scientist Presents Evidence for Belief* (New York: Free Press, 2006).

4. Kalonymus Kalmish Shapira, *Sacred Fire* (New York: Jason Aronson, 2002).

5. Mordecai Kaplan, *The Meaning of God in Modern Jewish Religion* (New York: Jewish Publication Society, 1962), 76.

6. Harold Kushner, *Nine Essential Things I've Learned About God* (New York: Random House, 2016), 44.

7. Karff, *Permission to Believe*, viii.

2. Texts

1. Attributed to Rabbi Louis Finkelstein, quoted in Marc Wolf, "The Question That Matters," April 12, 2003, www.jtsa.edu/the-question-that-matters.

2. Albert Einstein, *The World As I See It* (London: John Lane, The Bodley Head, 1934).

3. Steven Gimbel, *Einstein's Jewish Science: Physics at the Intersection of Politics and Religion* (Baltimore: Johns Hopkins University Press, 2013), 96.

3. Election, or God's Jedi Masters

1. See Robert D. Putnam and David E. Campbell, *American Grace: How Religion Divides and Unites Us* (New York: Simon & Schuster, 2012).

2. Babylonian Talmud, Tractate *Brachot*, 5a.

3. See "The Guiding Principles of Reform Judaism," Central Conference of American Rabbis, 1937, www.ccarnet.org/rabbinic-voice/platforms/article-guiding-principles-reform-judaism/.

4. Arnold Eisen, *The Chosen People in America* (Bloomington: Indiana University Press, 1983).

5. Emil Fackenheim, "Faith in God and Man After Auschwitz: Theological Implications," Holocaust Teacher Resource Center, June 3, 2002, www.holocaust-trc.org/faith-in-god-and-man-after-auschwitz-theological-implications/.

6. Joseph Stein, Sheldon Harnick, Jerry Bock et al., *Fiddler on the Roof* (New York: Times Square Music, 1964).

4. Israel

1. Quoted in Rabbi Daniel Glatstein, "You Shall Be Holy," TorahAnytime.com, May 14, 2016, www.torahanytime.com/#/post?id=35183.

2. Interview on CBS (5 October 1956).

3. See the website for Birthright Israel at www.birthrightisrael.com.

4. Babylonian Talmud, Tractate *Sanhedrin*, 72a.

5. See "AJC 2018 Survey of American & Israeli Jewish Opinion," American Jewish Committee, June 10, 2018, www.ajc .org/news/ajc-comparative-surveys-of-israeli-us-jews-show-some -serious-divisions.

5. The Calendar: Autumn Holidays

1. Samson Raphael Hirsch, quoted in Arthur Spier, *The Comprehensive Jewish Calendar* (New York: Feldheim, 1986), ix.

2. Joshua Stanton, "3 Unexpected Things I Did on the Day Rosh Hashanah and 9/11 Coincided," Wisdom Daily, September 12, 2018, http://thewisdomdaily.com/3-unexpected-things-i-did -on-the-day-rosh-hashanah-and-9-11-coincided.

3. See Jonathan Sacks, "The Courage to Live with Uncertainty," October 12, 2015, http://rabbisacks.org/the-courage-to-live-with -uncertainty/.

6. The Calendar: Winter and Spring Holidays

1. Martin Luther King Jr., sermon delivered at Temple Israel of Hollywood, February 26, 1965, www.americanrhetoric.com /speeches/mlktempleisraelhollywood.htm.

2. Jennifer Schultz, "Veterans by the Numbers," The National Conference of State Legislatures blog, November 10, 2017, www .ncsl.org/blog/2017/11/10/veterans-by-the-numbers.aspx.

7. Prayer

1. Joseph Soloveitchik, *The Lonely Man of Faith*, essay originally published in 1961, reissued in book form, (New York: Random House, 2009).

8. Everyday Holiness

1. Rabbi Twerski's discussion of this can be found at www .chabad.org/library/article_cdo/aid/1235774/jewish/My-Mothers -Candle-for-Me.htm.

2. Babylonian Talmud, Tractate *Menachot*, 43b.

3. Babylonian Talmud, Tractate *Berachot*, 35 a-b.

10. The Eternal Questions

1. Jonathan Sacks, "Did You Ask a Good Question Today?" Aish.com, Nov. 7, 2009, www.aish.com/sp/ph/68197797.html.

2. Shmuley Boteach, *Kosher Jesus* (Jerusalem: Gefen, 2012), 51.

3. George R. Berlin, *Defending the Faith: Nineteenth Century American Jewish Writings on Christianity and Jesus* (Albany: State University of New York Press, 1989), 141.

4. Shaul Magid, "The New Jewish Reclamation of Jesus in Late Twentieth-Century America," in Zev Garber, ed. *The Jewish Jesus: Revelation, Reflection, Reclamation* (West Lafayette, IN: Purdue University Press, 2011), 365.

5. Central Conference of American Rabbis (CCAR), "Declaration of Principles," 1885, www.ccarnet.org/rabbinic-voice/platforms/article-declaration-principles/.

6. *Avot d'Rabbi Natan* 31b., www.sefaria.org/Avot_D'Rabbi_Natan?lang=bi.

7. CCAR, "Declaration of Principles."

8. The most comprehensive study of American Jewry over the last decade was conducted by the Pew Research Center in 2013, www.pewforum.org/2013/10/01/jewish-american-beliefs-attitudes-culture-survey/.

9. Charles Duhigg, *The Power of Habit: Why We Do What We Do in Life and Business* (New York: Random House, 2012).

10. Brad Young, *Jesus the Jewish Theologian* (Grand Rapids: Baker, 1993), ix.